Beginner's Gu

Ottoman Embroidery

Joyce I Ross

SEARCH PRESS

Hand-made pottery plate 41 cm (16 in) in diameter, made in Kutahya, Turkey by M. Hvrak in 1993.

First published in Great Britain 2005

Search Press Limited
Wellwood, North Farm Road,
Tunbridge Wells, Kent TN2 3DR

Photographs by Alan Ross
Charts and diagrams by Joyce I Ross and Alan Ross

First published 2005 in New Zealand by David Bateman Ltd,
30 Tarndale Grove, Albany, Auckland, New Zealand

ISBN 1 84448 134 4

The Publishers and author can accept no responsibility for any consequences arising from the information, advice or instructions given in this publication.

Readers are permitted to reproduce any of the embroideries/ patterns in this book for their personal use, or for the purposes of selling for charity, free of charge and without the prior permission of the Publishers. Any use of the embroideries/patterns for commercial purposes is not permitted without the prior permission of the Publishers.

Suppliers
If you have difficulty in obtaining any of the materials and equipment mentioned in this book, please visit the Search Press website for details of suppliers: www.searchpress.com

Alternatively, you can write to the Publishers at the address above for a current list of stockists, which includes firms who operate a mail-order service.

Cover design Shelley Watson/Sublime Design
Book design Karen Moss/Purrfect Grafix
Printed in China through Colorcraft Ltd.

Acknowledgements

I acknowledge, with gratitude, the work of Valerie Candy and Elizabeth Dench, who stitched some of the projects detailed in this book from my notes alone, and members of my classes for their stimulation and encouragement.

During my studies, I have met many interesting people who have shared their stories and their treasures with me. Their names can be found throughout the book; without them there would have been no book.

I must also thank my husband Alan whose beautiful photography enhances this book. Alan accompanied me on all my journeys, taught our computer to jump through hoops and has nursed it back to sanity on many occasions. He has spent many hours helping me to 'computerise' this script.

Joyce I Ross, 2005.

Note: *Unless otherwise stated, all the embroideries are the original work of the author. The Ottoman goldwork known as dival embroidery is not included in this book due to its similarity to more universal forms of couched and laid work.*

Contents

Introduction

In September 1997 my husband Alan and I visited Turkey, the cradle of civilisation. One of our aims was to find the grave of Alan's Uncle Jim who was killed in the battle on the Gallipoli peninsula in November 1915. We walked through a field of red tomatoes to a beautifully kept little cemetery, where we found Uncle Jim's grave amongst 640 others of soldiers from Australia, New Zealand and Great Britain.

Some years later, with the impression of the scene still fresh in my mind, I made my iconic picture, 'Tribute' (see opposite page). A photograph of Uncle Jim was printed onto fine cotton. The mount of embroidered canvas-work was the background scene as I remembered it — brilliantly clear water in turquoise and sapphire blue, yellow sand, green scrub.

The stitches I used reminded me of the wonderful medieval mosaics made of small squares of coloured or gold-backed glass that we saw in the Hagia Sophia in Istanbul. The 'hunchback' poppies reminded me of the tomatoes at Gallipoli, and their shape was taken from a towel which had been picked up at Gallipoli in 1915, now held at the Auckland Museum. The poppy leaves were of Turkish triangular stitch using heavy metal thread.

As often happens in our searching, we find hidden treasures we never knew existed, and that is what happened to me during our journey through Turkey. We travelled through city and countryside, saw the urban sprawl of squatters' dwellings, plastic tents of itinerant gypsies, goat-hair tents of nomads, cotton fields and ripening fruit, ancient ruins untarnished by time in that arid climate, and modern museums.

We experienced apple tea, wonderful bread, luscious fruit, and food incompatibility. We explored cave dwellings and stayed in their modern-day equivalent, a hotel with wavy floors, low arched doorways and labyrinthine passages. We met schoolgirls practising their English. We visited a carpet factory and a pottery works, and brought back permanent memories. We did not see much embroidery apart from goldwork palls in some of the mosques.

I decided to study Turkish embroidery. Following a method of studying historic embroideries described in a booklet from the Embroiderers' Guild in the UK, the search began. I looked up 'Turkey' in every index in our local guild's library and found very little.

The breakthrough came after speaking at an Embroiderers' Guild meeting when a member lent me Ulla Thur's book, *Floral Messages*. I was hooked. Auckland's public library had three books on the topic. I devoured them all, working samples and learning some of the stitches. After hearing of the exhibition 'Flowers of Silk and Gold' at The Textile Museum in Washington D.C., I obtained the catalogue written by the exhibition curator, Sumru Belger Krody.

In 2000 a travel grant from the Association

'TRIBUTE'
13/194 James Alexander Ross
1892–1915

of New Zealand Embroiderers' Guilds enabled me to study some of the articles in Washington after the exhibition had been disassembled.

The use of the word 'Ottoman' produces a few problems. During the 400 years of Ottoman domination, Christians, Muslims, Jews, Turks, Greeks and Armenians lived in mutually supportive relationships throughout much of the Mediterranean region while continuing their particular cultural characteristics. Thus embroidery made by Greeks living in Turkey up until the 1920s is sometimes referred to as 'Ottoman'. I have restricted my researches to Turkish Ottoman embroidery. It is my hope that this book, as well as stimulating interest in Ottoman embroidery, will encourage embroiderers everywhere to look at the historical treasures we all have around us.

The search for Ottoman embroideries

It's always a good idea to see what you can find close to home. The Auckland Museum possesses only one piece of Ottoman embroidery. It is a Turkish towel, 'picked up at Gallipoli in 1915', and that is all the museum knows about it.

This is obviously not the work of a suburban workshop — more likely a towel lovingly made by a woman for her son, husband or sweetheart. It shows the typical 'hunchback' spray with flowers that was popular from 1850 onwards. The stems, dots and centres are probably silver gilt plate; the green leaves are probably chemically dyed silk thread. The flowers have faded from their original pink which is still visible in places.

The 'hunchback' style is an adaptation of the commonly found left-leaning orientation of floral sprays, 'wafting in Allah's heavenly breeze'. To the Ottomans every aspect of life was infused with their Islamic faith, hence the limitation of subject matter. Nothing with a soul, not even an insect, could be portrayed, and each flower had a significance that is now lost to us. The meanings were hidden in rhyme, for example, 'armit', the pear, rhymes with 'ümit', hope. Therefore the pear can mean 'give me hope'.

Turkish Towel from Gallipoli, 1915.
AUCKLAND WAR MEMORIAL MUSEUM

Treasures from the Second World War

After speaking to a group of embroiderers, I was approached by a lady from the audience who told me that she and her friend had collections of embroideries like the ones that I was describing. Subsequently Alan and I visited Margaret Boyce and Betty Reed and photographed both of their collections. To my great joy, Betty gave me two yagliks, or towels, one of which, the 'hollyhock' yaglik, is featured later in the book.

The value to me of having these traditional embroideries has been inestimable as I have been able to scrutinise them intimately. Margaret and Betty had been sent to Thrace by CORSO (the Council of Organisations for Relief Services Overseas) at the end of the Second World War, and they had found these embroideries for sale at the local markets.

This yaglik was purchased in Komitini, a market town with a population of about 5,000. MARGARET BOYCE COLLECTION

19th-century yaglik, the tree pattern of which has been unchanged for 400 years. MARGARET BOYCE COLLECTION

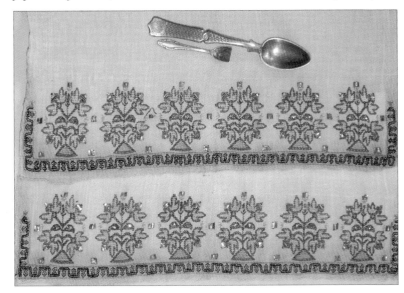

A yaglik with a Turkish silver teaspoon and caviar spoon. MARGARET BOYCE COLLECTION

Historical background

During my initial reading, I became familiar with only 18th- and 19th-century Ottoman embroideries. In Washington D.C. I discovered that these are referred to as 'Ottoman Rococo' style, which grew out of the Westernisation of a vibrant indigenous style, the French influence being particularly strong. As I studied further, I realised that these embroideries gave a wonderful window into the changing culture that produced them.

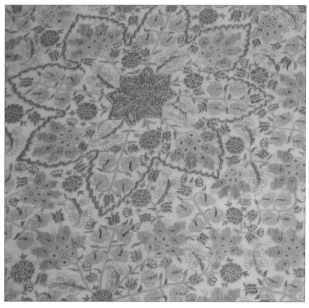

The centre of the cover is an eight-point floral star, surrounded by eight 'petals'. From each of the corners, identical floral sprays radiate towards the centre. In the centre of each side is a similar floral spray, thus completely covering the square with stitching. The embroidery is mostly in Romanian couching. The cotton fabric was joined before being embroidered with silk threads in light and dark greens, blue, two pinks, cream, beige, yellow and silver wound on yellow silk. WITH PERMISSION FROM THE OTAGO MUSEUM

The collection in Washington, which spanned 400 years, mirrored the changing lifestyle of the Ottomans as other cultures influenced them. Originally a nomadic people, the Ottomans had to bundle everything up and pack it into saddlebags every time they moved, which was often. Looms were small and collapsible. The fabric produced on them was usually about 45 cm (18 in) wide. If a larger piece of cloth was required, as for a turban cover, pieces were joined, either before or after embroidery.

As there was no paper in that hot dry climate, precious things, like turbans, had to be wrapped against dust. These wrappings were always embroidered. Money payments were often made wrapped in embroidered handkerchiefs.

For the nomad, the tent served as bedroom, living room and kitchen. Ottoman Turks were an inherently artistic people — they lived close to the earth, knew the cycle of the seasons intimately, understood how to dye wool with plant extracts, and observed the colours of the world around them. They are well known for their magnificent carpets, and their embroideries are no less beautiful.

In 1453 the Ottomans conquered Constantinople, the capital of the Byzantine Empire and the most magnificent city in Europe, which in earlier days had been the

capital of the eastern Roman Empire. They must have loved the colour and opulence of the city they had taken.

As they settled into urban living, they built their houses like tents with multi-purpose rooms. They loved the Italian brocades, but could not weave them on their little looms. They had silk, since the introduction of Chinese mulberry trees years before, and silk could be dyed with the same plant dyes as wool, as it too is an animal protein. They grew cotton and could weave it, but cotton is hard to dye, requiring chemical mordants, the source and use of which the nomads would have had no knowledge.

So, ever resourceful, the Ottomans stitched the brocades they so admired in bright pure colours. The earliest surviving embroideries I saw were 17th century. These were mirror covers and lined floor mats (placed underneath the tray of food at meal times, twice a day). In the 18th century, the purpose, and therefore the style and the stitches, changed to produce articles that were the same front and back. The stitches that make this possible are mainly double running stitch and Turkish triangular stitch. Musabak stitch is the pulled version of Turkish triangular stitch, and it was used frequently in later embroideries.

This red woollen cover, Catalogue F89.56, embroidered in chain stitch with a tambour hook — because of its great regularity — is believed to be 20th century. It is approximately 100 cm (39 in) square. It is worked in shades of green, cream and blue with silver wire wrapped on white silk. As with the previous cover, each part of the design radiates towards the eight-part central portion. A similar cover, Catalogue T126, exists in the Victoria & Albert Museum, London, embroidered on red silk. WITH PERMISSION FROM THE OTAGO MUSEUM

Border of a yaglik. MARGERY BLACKMAN COLLECTION

Features of the embroideries

It became obvious very early from my readings that there are several distinctive features of these embroideries. The embroideries originated in the royal palaces of Bursa and Istanbul, from whence they spread to the provinces as far away as Morocco, carried by the wives of Ottoman ambassadors, administrators and high-ranking army officers. A harem-trained wife was often given to a faithful official as a reward. Much of the embroidery was done by women and eunuchs in the harems. By the mid-18th century the fashion had changed and embroidered napkins, sashes, head scarves, turban wrappers and bath towels were in more common use. As demand soon outgrew supply, urban workshops were set up in the two major cities. Metal thread-makers were also employed, their job being to wind gold or silver gilt wire onto silk of varying shades.

Not many of the early mirror covers and hangings still exist. No doubt they wore out but there is evidence that some articles were recycled.

Trees and Houses. This towel is worked mainly in musabak stitch — the attempt at perspective in the foreground probably dates it as late 19th century. MARGARET BOYCE COLLECTION

Subject matter

In accordance with Ottoman faith, nothing with a soul could be portrayed, although in the late 19th century we do see the appearance of little birds, thought to represent the soul, and even a camel. However, not all the embroiderers would have been Muslim. The very earliest piece of Ottoman embroidery is found on the top of a pair of 17th-century riding boots embellished with gold stitchery, but during my studies I saw only hangings, floor mats and covers of various kinds from that era.

Abstract plant forms were always the basis of the repeating patterns. Later, realistic plant forms, houses and gardens, fruit and boats appeared, and in the 20th century familiar animals were portrayed.

Signature on a silk organza tunic. PATSY ARMSTRONG COLLECTION

It is no surprise that the Ottomans, being historically nomadic people, retained their affection for tents, the images of which occur frequently in Ottoman embroideries. These varied from simple outdoor pavilions, the designs of which are very similar to modern-day ones that can be purchased in chain stores, to more elaborate 'travelling palaces'. The Ottomans were forever on the move, with a huge empire that required constant attention and frequent wars. *Hali* magazine, No. 37, Jan–Feb 1988, has an excellent descriptive article about these large-scale tents.

Ciphers, being works of art in themselves, can be found on clothing, and there is a beautiful script on a divan cover at 'Olveston', an Edwardian mansion in Dunedin, New Zealand. The divan cover is from Egypt, another Ottoman province. The ciphers were copied from the coinage of the time.

Designs

The earliest Ottoman embroideries on cloth were made to emulate Italian brocades, and the designs were derived from plant forms. The Ottomans adapted many symbols from the countries with which they came into contact during their travels. Thus we see shapes like the Buddhist 'flaming pearl', sometimes described as the badge of Tamerlane who temporarily shattered Ottoman rule in Asia Minor. The fish form on Chinese porcelain is adapted to palmate form on pottery plates to this day. I puzzled for ages over a little squiggle design stitched on a late 17th-century floor spread, until I

*Floral embroidery on a yaglik
40 x 100 cm (16 x 39 in).*
PATSY ARMSTRONG COLLECTION

saw a photograph of a 16th-century child's dress of silk and gold tissue woven with a device described as 'tiger stripes'. The floor spread also depicted the three-circle device of Tamerlane, and, according to the Victoria & Albert Museum's *Brief Guide to Turkish Woven Fabrics*, these symbols often occur together.

We see the 'Paisley' or 'pine cone' symbols from Persia, and we also see the unique shapes of the country they knew so well, such as the carnation, the needle-point petals of the tulip and the crown-shaped stylised hyacinth.

In most early examples, the motifs are neither inverted nor rotated, but march boldly along the length or breadth of the article. There are many similar examples in existence, the differences lying in the individual way big spaces are filled in. It's almost as if the embroiderer, when faced with a big area to cover with, for example, pattern darning, put lots of interesting detail within the shape to break the monotony of the one type of stitch. The in-fill spray of flowers, or stalk of tulips, or branch of twigs, or daisy chain certainly make big leaves more lively and interesting to look at as well as to stitch.

The intensity of colour chosen for any piece of work can alter the balance of the composition. Every woman knows that dark colours create a slim silhouette and that horizontal stripes are sure to increase apparent girth. In early examples, imbalance in design was corrected by adding blobs of embroidery, which is a very painterly way of working. The women and men who stitched these embroideries were natural artists.

With increasing urbanisation and Western influence, the need for sophisticated domestic embroidery grew, hence the increasingly elaborate napkins of varying sizes used at meal times, and the elegant Turkish towels used at the public baths. We owe our existing bath towels to the Ottomans, for they developed articles with embroidered ends and loop pile for greater absorption. We use towels today of loop pile cotton with borders of flat woven fabric a few centimetres from the ends. These borders serve no useful purpose whatsoever, except to remind us of the towel's origin.

Sprays of flowers, which became more realistic as the centuries passed, were always depicted as 'swaying in Allah's heavenly breeze'. Favourite trees and fruits as well as flowers were subjects for embroidery. Later, houses and tents, pavilions and urns of flowers (the 'tree of life' motif) and boats began to appear. By the 19th century subjects such as camels carrying coffins and birds on a gravestone (I have seen a similar pattern in Assisi embroidery) indicate the increasing secularisation of Turkish society, even before the fall of the Sultans.

Colour palette

The earliest Ottoman embroideries on fabric were embroidered in strong pure colours of yellow, red, blue and green, and they were worked on very flimsy cotton or cotton-linen mix. By the mid-18th century, colours had become muted: pastel pinks and blues were the favourites. Metal wires wound on silk cores of varying colours gave subtlety to the embroideries.

We can learn much about colour usage from a study of articles from this era. The embroiderers obviously observed nature acutely, for we see the colour of a rosebud echoed in its leaves, the shading of a full-blown rose realistically simulated using double running stitch. However, colours are not always derived from nature, or are

they? Grapes in late 18th-century articles, for example, are always depicted as yellow. Why? Purple and mauve were not favoured colours, or perhaps the embroiderers did not have plants that yielded those shades. Certain shellfish produce purple dye, but this would not have been in common use, especially inland away from the coast. I understand that grapes were specially bred in Turkey as a table fruit, and they were yellow.

Understanding the plant dyes that were used to make silk threads is an area beyond the scope of this book.

Stitches

17th to early 18th centuries

- ꙮ Pattern darning — worked horizontally, vertically or diagonally
- ꙮ Atma stitch — worked over unspun silk
- ꙮ Chain stitch
- ꙮ Double running stitch
- ꙮ Turkish triangular stitch
- ꙮ Herringbone and fishbone stitches
- ꙮ Bukhara and Romanian couching

From the late 18th century

- ꙮ Double running stitch
- ꙮ Satin stitch, buttonhole stitch
- ꙮ Musabak stitch
- ꙮ Murver stitch
- ꙮ Chain stitch — design on the back of the fabric, made with a tambour hook
- ꙮ Cross stitch

Outlining the pattern

It appears that the pattern was marked on the fabric, front or back, which indicates that the stitchery was sometimes worked from the reverse. Historically, designs were drawn in Indian ink.

Sometimes motifs were outlined in black stitches. If these outlines are still visibly black today, the outline would have been made with human hair; if the outline is now rusty red, the original black would probably have been created by soaking iron filings in vinegar; these of course rusted with age and the silk decayed.

Modern edges on linen Cocktail napkins purchased in Washington D.C. in 2002. AUTHOR'S COLLECTION

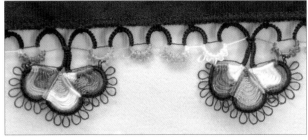

Modern edge on one side of a black polyester scarf, 132 x 76 cm (52 x 30 in). DONNA KENNEDY COLLECTION

Unusual edging on a yaglik. MARGERY BLACKMAN COLLECTION

Edges

Ottoman embroidered towels and sashes were made of hand-woven strips of cotton or cotton-linen fabric created on narrow looms. Thus only the top and bottom edges needed to be finished in some way. The weave was 19 threads per centimetre (48 threads per inch), which is much finer than most people find comfortable to stitch today. The embroideries in this book are designed for 10 or 11 threads per centimetre (26 or 29 threads per inch), and there is the problem for us of what to do with the long edges as modern fabrics are woven on a wide loom. Ottoman towels, floor mats and turban covers were joined either before or after embroidery. They were finished in a variety of ways: most commonly a simple rolled hem, or sometimes crocheted in metal threads, or a frayed edge, and occasionally an irregularly scalloped edge neatly finished with buttonhole stitch.

Needle lace edging. Detail of silk organza tunic showing needle lace edge motif (oya) made of detached buttonhole stitch with metal thread inclusions. PATSY ARMSTRONG COLLECTION

A detailed study: The 'hollyhock' yaglik

This 19th-century towel — I call it the 'hollyhock' yaglik — has five motifs across its 45 cm (18 in) width, and the side borders only come up as far as the top of the motifs. I have no proof other than instinct that it was made in the second half of the 19th century because of the use of gold plate.

There are eight glorious colours — deep and mid pink, pink beige, dull blue, dark and light green, khaki and a pinky grey — with silver gilt wound on yellow silk metal thread as well as the gold plate. There is alternate use of mid pink and pink beige in the flowers. At the top of each 'tree' there is a tiny, deep pink circular flower in buttonhole stitch. The 'mound' is in khaki musabak stitch, and the 'leaves' in Turkish triangular stitch in the two greens with dull blue central veins.

The 19th century
'hollyhock' yaglik
45 x 84 cm (18 x 33 in).
BETTY REED COLLECTION

15

The entire embroidery has the classical dimensions of 45 x 84 cm (18 x 33 in). The fabric was woven on a small loom. The long sides, being selvedges, needed no further finishing, and the short ends have been hemmed by rolling the fine fabric in the fingers and securing it with tiny stitches.

Close inspection shows that the stitches employed were musabak for the mound, self-couching for the flowers, Turkish triangular for the foliage, and double saw tooth for the 'trunk' of the pinky grey and blue 'trees'. Fishbone stitch in gold plate was used for the larger flower centres and satin stitch in the same gold plate for the smaller centres.

How was the double saw tooth stitch made? Experimentation with herringbone and double-sided cross stitches did not prove to be satisfactory. I found the best rendition was to use the threads doubled in the needle (refer to the description for double saw tooth stitch in the dictionary of stitches).

For weeks I struggled with self-couching, looking at all the books I could find with it listed, and then I simply developed a technique. I made a series of evenly spaced sloping stitches over two threads of fabric. Then the same thread was carried through all the stitches, the work turned over and threaded through the stitches on the reverse side to give the same appearance on both sides of the fabric.

While some patterns in Ottoman embroidery remained unchanged over hundreds of years, individuality in stitches did appear. Murver stitch appears to have been made in a variety of ways, only one of which is shown in the dictionary of stitches (see page

A flower motif from the 'hollyhock' yaglik.

Magnification of the 'tree' portion of the 'hollyhock' yaglik.

30). It is quite possible that embroiderers, like artists, then as now, had unique ways of making marks.

The realisation that much of the stitchery was Turkish triangular came as a surprise, as I thought that by the late 19th century it had been replaced with musabak or murver stitches. The magnification opposite shows quite clearly how much thicker the embroidery thread was than that of the background fabric.

We study and admire historical embroideries but find it neither desirable nor possible to copy them exactly. Everything we then stitch becomes an interpretation. The fabric, threads and tools are different, and possibly five years hence some of the threads I have used will no longer be available.

This process has gone on continually.

Ottoman embroideries of the 18th century show an increasing Western influence, particularly from France, and likewise European art was influenced by Ottoman art. First William Morris, then later the artists of the Art Nouveau era and its offspring, the Art Deco era of the 1920s, drew heavily on the Ottoman Rococo style. The other interesting feature of this period is the total disregard for scale and the attractive blend of big and little — by no means the preserve of Ottoman embroideries. The same characteristics are found in illuminated manuscripts from the Middle Ages.

'Beside Sweet Waters' is a picture inspired by the 'Trees and Houses' yaglik on page 10. I used the tree I 'discovered' in the hollyhock yaglik and added oversized roses on either side of the main building. 'Sweet Waters' was an area between two streams flowing into the Golden Horn, Istanbul – prime real estate.

General guidelines

The materials used in Ottoman embroidery are generally available from good needlework shops. Specialist materials are available from mail order outlets who advertise in the needlework magazines.

Fabrics

Ottoman embroideries were stitched on a tight frame in silk on cotton or a cotton-linen mix, usually 45 cm (18 in) wide with 19 stitches per cm (48 threads per in). Modern Turkish embroideries are worked on commercially produced fabrics (you can see the yellow and black selvedge lines in the illustration below and also on page 69). I have found it convenient to use a linen fabric with 10 or 11 threads per cm (26 or 29 threads per in), making sure that it is suitable for pulled fabric work if murver or musabak stitches are to be used.

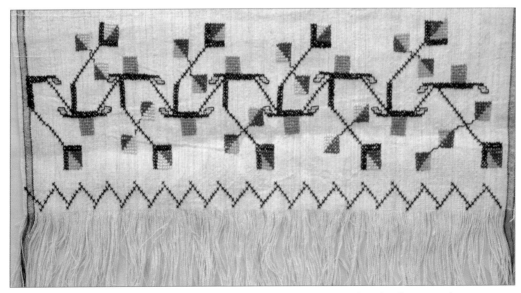

Modern table scarf. This embroidery, 120 x 39 cm (47 x 15 in), with 14 cm (5.5 in) deep frayed ends, was made on commercially produced fabric and is late 20th century. It is embroidered entirely in cross stitch and it shows most of the characteristics of typical Turkish domestic embroidery — the colours, the type of design, the border and dimensions. DONNA KENNEDY COLLECTION

Threads

Ottoman embroiderers used silk threads and metal wires — gold, silver, silver gilt, and copper — wound on pastel-coloured silk filaments to give great subtlety of colour. The number of colours used in 18th-century embroideries varied between four and sixteen. The colours are various shades of blue, red, pink, yellow, green, orange, brown, cream as well as black (human hair) and white.

From the mid-19th century, metal plate was used, often simply threaded through the fabric, but in Turkish punch stitch the technique of using a needle and securing each stitch separately was perfected.

The easiest threads to work with are mono-filament, such as perle cotton and mulberry silks, but a greater range of colours is available in stranded cottons, or floss, and in rayon stranded threads.

During the 1970s, when Turkish fashion clothing was embellished with embroidery, Springers Marlitt, a shiny rayon thread, was used. Rayon thread is difficult to control and I find damping it slightly is helpful.

Suitable metallic thread substitutes are DMC perle for heavier fabrics such as canvas (6 threads per cm/14 threads per in) and several stranded threads, including two gold shades, copper and silver, that can be split. Some lurex-type machine-embroidery threads work well, and on canvas even quite heavy threads will go through a needle and look quite effective.

Gold-coloured plate, used in Ottoman embroideries from the 19th century, is more difficult to obtain, but I find an acceptable thick thread to be Glamour metallic Madeira. It is sometimes sold in wool shops and has two shades of gold in its range. There are other exciting composite threads put out by small boutique enterprises.

Thread thickness

For fabrics with 10 or 11 threads per cm (26 or 29 threads per in), use two or three strands of stranded cotton (or floss), or one strand of Marlitt and one of cotton. Two strands of Marlitt and two strands of Madeira silk are thicker than two strands of ordinary stranded cotton.

Pattern darning stitch:
use two strands of floss or No. 8 perle.

Bukhara and Romanian couching:
use six strands of floss or No. 5 perle.

Atma stitch:
use six strands of floss or No. 5 perle for the couching and any thick thread for the single-faced satin stitch.

Turkish triangular stitch:
use two or three strands of floss or No. 8 perle.

Musabak and murver stitches:
use one or two strands of floss or No. 8 perle.

Double running as a filling stitch:
use two or three strands of floss on fabrics with 10 threads per cm (26 threads per in) and two strands of floss on fabric with 11 per cm (29 threads per in).

Double running as an edging:
use two strands of floss or gold DMC perle split in half.

Borders

Embroidered ends had narrow border patterns close to the main field. The border patterns came up the long sides of the article as far as the top of the main pattern. Not much thought was given to the corners, as can be seen from the examples, possibly because many of the embroiderers were without things like rulers and tape measures. Sometimes the design flowed effortlessly round the corner, but this is more common in the later examples that I have seen.

The border patterns in themselves are fascinating. They usually relate to the main motifs, and the colour distribution in the small flowers is not alternate. The side border patterns are missing from the late 20th-century embroideries that I have seen.

Edges

The problem of the long edges in towels and sashes did not arise historically. Embroideries from the 17th century onwards were made on narrow weaving looms, and were simply hemmed on the narrow ends; the other two sides were selvedges. Narrow pieces were joined together, before or after embroidery, to make covers, valances and floor mats. All the edges were hemmed close to the narrow border. Occasionally the very edge was finished with crochet using metal wire, and some examples show simple needle lace or buttonhole stitch around complex curves.

Modern Turkish domestic embroideries appear to be made on commercially produced narrow fabrics. Unless you can obtain some of this narrow fabric, you may have a problem (possible solutions are given in the project for a collection of Ottoman borders and motifs on page 57.

Hints

- When using metallic threads I find it helpful to run the thread through a piece of beeswax before starting to stitch.

- Double running stitches around floral motifs, leaves and stems look best if made with tiny stitches over two and under two threads, being careful to round off the design. Make no abrupt changes in direction.

- Designs were originally drawn on with a brush and Indian ink. Use a waterproof fibre-tip pen and trace using a light-box.

- Always work in an embroidery frame.

- Use a size 26 tapestry needle. When darning in ends use a sharp needle.

- Always begin by leaving a 'tail' that you can darn in later.

- In the earliest embroideries, stitching around the motifs was either absent or done in brown, black, or a contrasting colour. In later embroideries edgings were in gold or the same as one of the colours in the detail. When in doubt use gold, and make satin stitch surrounds wide enough to be able to darn in start and finish 'tails'.

- Complete the edges of the motifs last.

- When ironing your embroidery, place it face-down on a soft pad and use a piece of baking paper between the iron and your embroidery. Remember that the metal threads are probably of the lurex type and may melt.

Dictionary of stitches

Being situated between east and west, a great variety of stitches were appropriated in Ottoman embroideries.

What makes this art form so intriguing is that the simple, earliest stitches of pattern darning and the unique Turkish triangular stitch evolved into the double sided stitches of double running, murver and musabak.

Together with gold and silver wire wound on silk and thread through a needle, these stitches produced glorious articles for domestic use.

Wall hanging, designed by author and stitched by Valerie Candy.

Alma stitch

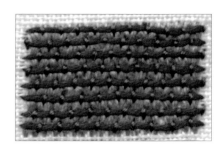

This stitch is described in several ways, depending on which book you are following. Sometimes the stitch is called 'laid and couched stitch', which describes it well. Essentially, rows of single-faced satin stitch are laid down, traditionally in unspun silk. These are secured with a variation of Bukhara self-couching, in rows spaced out to allow the underlying one-faced satin stitch to show. The method described here employs three different weights and colours of threads for clarity. Marlitt is used here in place of unspun silk.

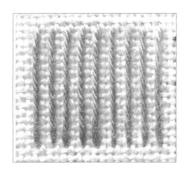

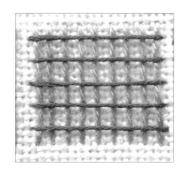

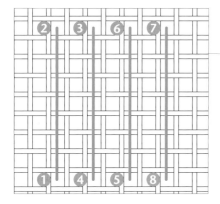

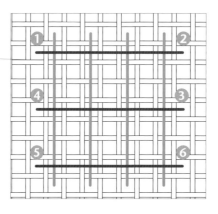

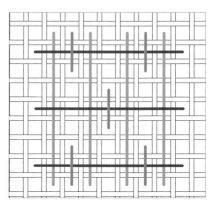

STEP 1
Make vertical rows of single-faced satin stitch. Bring the needle up at 1 on one edge of the area to be stitched, and insert it at 2 on the opposite edge. Miss a hole, bring the needle up at 3, and make another stitch by inserting the needle at 4. Continue as shown.

STEP 2
Secure the vertical rows with long horizontal rows of single-faced satin stitch, three fabric threads apart. Bring the needle up at 1 for the first stitch, insert the needle at 2, miss two holes, and bring the needle back up at 3 for the next stitch.

STEP 3
Couch this down with vertical stitches as shown.

Bukhara self-couching stitch (also spelt Bokhara and Boukhara)

As with atma stitch, there are many ways of describing this stitch — as there are ways of spelling it. The distinguishing feature of this form of couching is the short tying or couching stitches. The laid threads, which may be horizontal or slanting, are caught down ('couched') by short stitches which may be perpendicular or at an angle to the individual laid threads.

The traditional method is to make a long diagonal stitch across the area to be stitched, then, with the same needle and thread, return underneath, making small horizontal stitches at regular intervals on the front surface to secure the first long stitch. Continue to cover the area, staggering the securing stitches.

However, I have found that the best way to work the stitch is to make the row of tying stitches first.

STEP 1
Bring the needle up at 1, and insert it at 2; bring it up again at 3 and insert it at 4; and so on.

STEP 2
Now bring the needle to the front of the fabric again at the end of the row of tying stitches (7) and pass it under all of them.

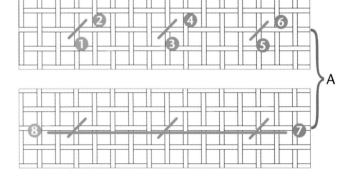

STEP 3
Secure the thread by taking it down into the fabric at 8, then bring it up again to commence a new row of tying stitches. If the fabric is too fine to count, guidelines may have to be drawn on it.

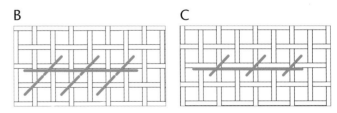

Alternative versions

B   C

Three versions of Bukhara self-couching stitch.

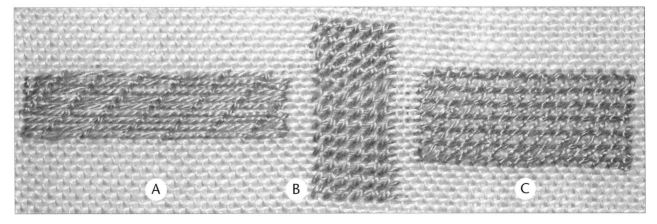

23

Buttonhole stitch

Buttonhole stitch worked over two warp threads, with two weft threads between each stitch. It is used as an edging in the projects in this book.

STEP 1
Bring the needle out of the fabric at 1 and insert it at 2 above the stitching line.

STEP 2
Bring the needle out at 3, ensuring the thread is looped under the needle (as shown).

Pull through and repeat.

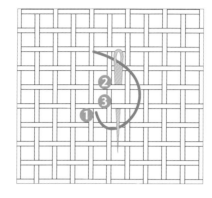 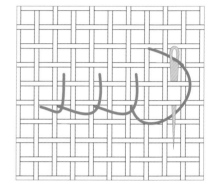

Chain stitch

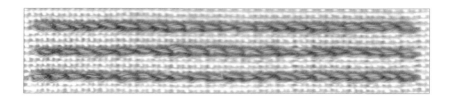

Many forms of embroidery use chain stitch

STEP 1
Bring the needle out at 1 and insert it into the fabric again at 1, leaving a loop of thread lying on top of the fabric.

Making a small downward stitch, bring the needle out at 2 but inside the loop.

STEP 2
Insert the needle at 3 (where you came up at 2), leaving a loop.

Make another small downward stitch, coming out at 4 inside the second loop.

STEP 3
Repeat as required. Complete the chain with a small stitch to secure the last loop.

Chain stitch in a variety of threads on denim.

Cross stitch

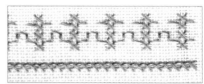

STEP 1

Make a row of diagonal stitches, up two and over two threads, working from left to right.

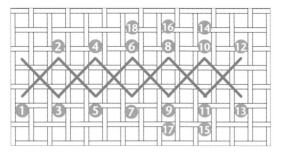

STEP 2

Turn and make a row of diagonal stitches from right to left.

Note

The stitch at the back of the fabric will be vertical.

This form of cross stitch is not reversible.

Detached buttonhole stitch

A version of this stitch is used in the Turkish 'oya' scarf or clothing edging, called 'bebila' in Greek, and in this book is used to cover the head of a tassel described in the lily cushion project (page 50).

STEP 1

Make a foundation row of double running stitch or chain stitch.

STEP 2

Bring the needle out at 1, and over the first stitch of the base row, then under that stitch, keeping the thread under the needle (as you would for a regular buttonhole stitch).

STEP 3

Leave a loose loop and slide the needle close to the fabric underneath the loop as shown.

STEP 4

Repeat.

The detached buttonhole stitch cap on the tassel of the lily cushion is worked round and round, so just keep going until the cap is as big as required.

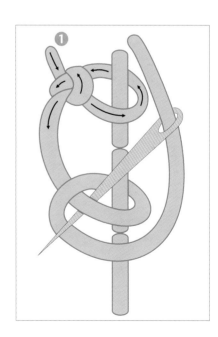

Dog tooth stitch

This stitch looks the same on the front as on the reverse of the fabric.

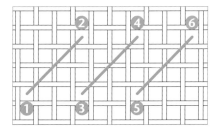 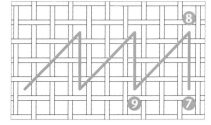

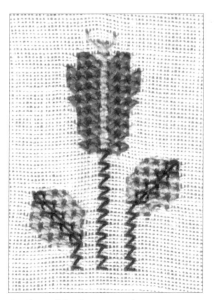

STEP 1
Make a row of diagonal stitches, up three and over three threads, working from left to right: bring the needle out of the fabric at 1 and insert it at 2, and so on.

STEP 2
Turn, and make a row of vertical stitches, up three threads, working from right to left: bring the needle out of the fabric at 7 and insert it at 8, and so on.

Stitch used for the stems only.

Double running stitch

This stitch is used for shading, working the darkest colour first. Sometimes it is necessary to change the direction of the stitches, to give the effect of petal or leaf shapes.

Examples of double running stitch. Can be used as filling stitches for large areas. The work is reversible.

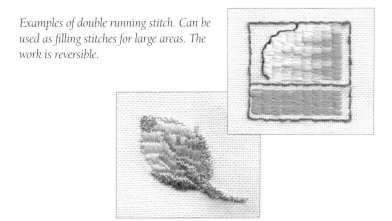

A 19th-century sash, 212 x 24.5 cm (83.5 x 9.5 in), with selvedges both sides, worked in double running and satin stitches. The threads are silk and gold wire wound on yellow silk, with both gold and silver plate. The border is encroaching Vandyke satin stitch, and the edge is a type of buttonhole stitch. PATSY ARMSTRONG COLLECTION

STEP 1
On the first row (working from left to right), work over and under the same number of threads each time.

Example shows over five threads.

STEP 2
On the return 'journey' (shown in orange), fill in the spaces, but be sure that you always bring the needle out of the fabric on the same side of the first-row stitch and take it into the fabric on the opposite side of the next stitch.

Double saw tooth stitch

The thread can be used doubled for this stitch.

STEP 1
Working left to right, make a row of diagonal stitches as shown: bring the needle out of the fabric at the odd numbers and insert it at the even numbers.

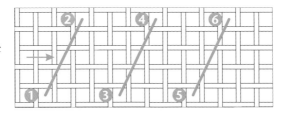

STEP 2
Return, working from right to left, and fill in the gaps with another row of diagonal stitches as shown: again, bring the needle out of the fabric at the odd numbers and insert it at the even numbers. This will complete a row of wave stitches (see page 39).

STEP 3
Reverse and make another row of wave stitches below the first row.

STEP 4
Make a row of double running stitches down the centre of the rows of wave stitches, as shown. Use the same holes in the fabric that you used for the wave stitches.

Only the trunk is in double saw tooth stitch — the foliage is Turkish triangular stitch.

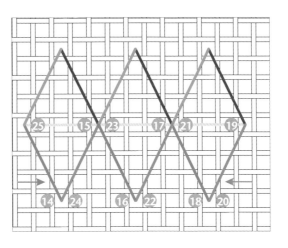

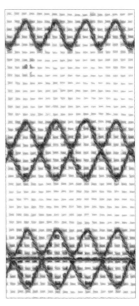

27

Double-sided cross stitch

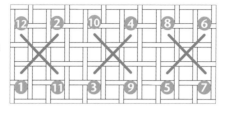

STEP 1

Working from left to right, make a row of diagonal stitches: bring the needle out at 1 and insert it at 2; bring the needle up at 3 (the stitch at the back of the fabric will be diagonal) and insert it at 4; repeat along the row.

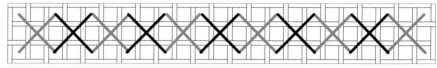

Note

This form of cross stitch is reversible, unlike the standard cross stitch.

STEP 2

Turn and make a similar row of diagonal stitches from right to left.

Fishbone stitch

This stitch is double-sided and ideal for small leaves. Work from the tip of the leaf to the base.

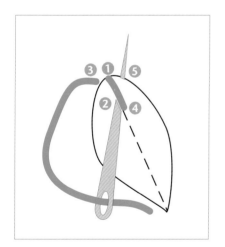

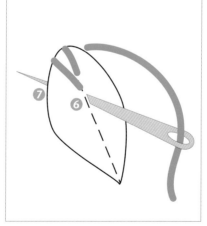

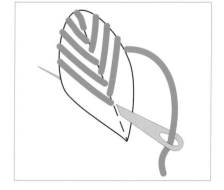

STEP 1

Bring the needle up at 1, insert it at 2, bring it up again at 3 as close as possible to the previous stitch. Insert it at 4 and bring up on the opposite side of the first stitch at 5.

STEP 2

Insert the needle at 6 (just below 4) to complete the first pair of stitches. Bring the needle up at 7 for the next stitch.

STEP 3

Continue making pairs of stitches left and right until the whole leaf is filled in, keeping the stitches close together.

Half cross stitch

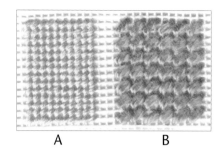

A   B

As the name suggests, this stitch is simply the first row of diagonal stitches without the 'crosses'.

In A, the half cross stitch has been worked up one end and over one thread of fabric. In B, as in the diagram, the stitch has been worked in a heavier perle thread, up two and over two threads of the fabric.

Bring the needle out at 1 and insert it at 2; bring the needle up at 3 (the stitch at the back of the fabric will be vertical) and insert it at 4; repeat along the row.

Hemstitching (Ottoman)

This is not used very often, but I have seen it on the short ends of table towels or yagliks as preparation for a needleweaving border. It is a three-sided stitch with the horizontal part below the drawn thread opening.

STEP 1 First prepare the rectangular area to be embroidered by withdrawing the required number of threads from the fabric. If you wish to embroider over the short ends with Ottoman hemstitching, make sure the number of threads you have withdrawn is a multiple of three.

STEP 2 At either end of the drawn area: either darn each of the drawn threads on the wrong side of the fabric, making each one finish at a different place, being careful not to pull the darned thread too tightly; or cut the drawn threads close to the edge of the area to be embroidered, then, using machine-thread the same colour as the background, stitch over the cut edge a few times.
These few stitches will be hidden by the hemstitching.

To work the hemstitching.

STEP 1 Bring the needle out of the framed area at the darned end at 1. Insert it into the fabric three threads lower at 2.

STEP 2 Pass the needle under the fabric three threads to the right to come out at 3.

STEP 3 Insert the needle into the fabric again at 4 (same hole as 2) then pass it diagonally behind the fabric (up three and over three threads) to come out at 5.

STEP 4 Insert the needle into the fabric three threads lower at 6 (same hole as 3).

STEP 5 Start the next stitch by bringing the needle out three threads horizontally along at 7.

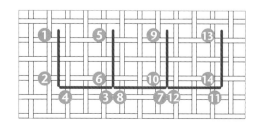

Herringbone stitch

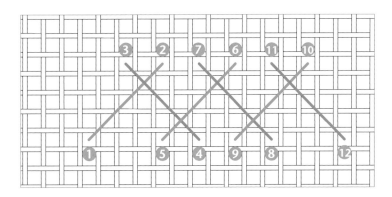

STEP 1

Bring the needle out of the fabric at 1.

Take it diagonally up four threads and across four threads to insert it into the fabric at 2; come back two threads and bring it out again at 3.

STEP 2

Take the needle diagonally (down four threads and across four threads to insert it into the fabric at 4; come back two threads horizontally and bring it out again at 5.

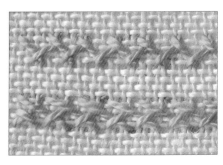

Repeat these diagonal stitches to make a row of interlocking crosses on the front of the fabric and two rows of parallel lines of stitches on the back.

Murver stitch

Murver stitch has been worked in a number of different ways over the centuries.

It must be worked in a frame. Each stitch should be pulled to give the effect shown. Unpulled murver stitch on canvas makes an attractive background filler.

Although not reversible, it looks attractive on the reverse side as well.

The base of each 'T' is the right-hand point of the previous 'T'.

STEP 1

Bring the needle out at the left-hand edge of the fabric at 1.

Make a stitch by inserting the needle at 2, four threads to the right.

Take the needle down two threads and back two threads, and bring it out of the fabric at 3.

Insert it again at 4, which is in the middle of and over the previous stitch being careful not to split the stitch.

Pass the needle vertically up two threads and bring it out at 5 to start the next stitch.

Repeat to form a diagonal row of ascending 'T's.

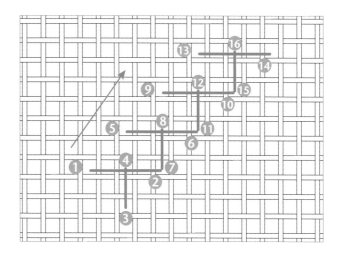

STEP 2

At the top of the first row, bring the needle out at the right-hand side of the last 'T' stitch (at 14).

Make a stitch by inserting the needle at 15, four threads to the left.

Take the needle up two threads and under two threads, and bring it out of the fabric at 16, directly above the centre of the long stitch.

Make a vertical stitch by inserting the needle at 17, which is in the middle of and over the previous stitch; again, be careful not to split the stitch.

Pass the needle vertically down two threads and bring it out at 18 to start the next stitch.

Repeat to form a diagonal row of descending 'T's close up to the ascending row (so that the horizontal stitches are double).

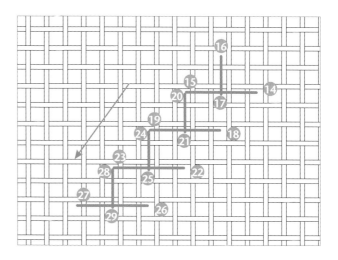

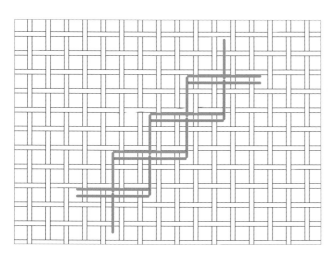

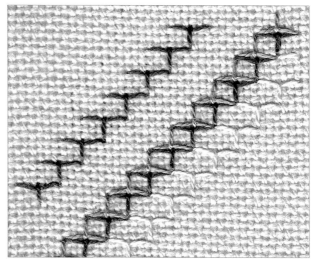

Murver stitch detail on linen (6 threads per cm/14 threads per in).

Musabak stitch

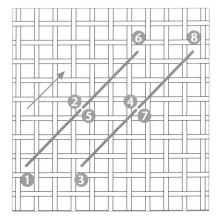

Musabak stitch must be worked in a frame. The central diagonal line of stitching will be doubled.

Each row should be pulled tight to give the effect shown. This unavoidably distorts the fabric.

STEP 1

Bring the needle out at 1 and make a diagonal stitch over three and up three threads, inserting the needle into the fabric at 2.

Pass the needle vertically down behind the fabric, and bring it out immediately below the end of the first stitch at 3.

Take the needle diagonally up three and across three and insert it into the fabric at 4 to make a diagonal stitch parallel to the first one.

Take the needle horizontally behind the fabric to come out at 5 at the top of the first stitch (the same hole as 2).

Repeat to form two rows of parallel diagonal stitches.

STEP 2

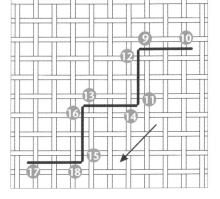

Take the needle horizontally behind the fabric to the top stitch of the parallel line of stitches (at 9); make a horizontal stitch on top of the fabric by inserting the needle at 10 (the top of the other parallel line of stitches).

Take the needle diagonally down behind the fabric to emerge at 11.

Make a vertical stitch on top by inserting the needle into the fabric at 12.

Take the needle diagonally down behind the fabric to emerge at 13 and make a horizontal stitch on top of the fabric by inserting the needle at 14.

Repeat these two stitches to finish at the start of row 1.

STEP 3

Repeat to form a second row.

Start at the bottom again, but three threads to the right (at 15 and 18).

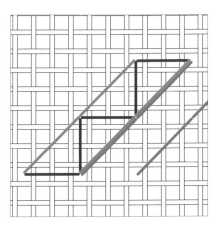

Needleweaving

First of all draw the threads and work Ottoman hemstitching around the work area.

This pattern in the stitched example is used in the collection of Ottoman motifs and borders (page 57).

STEP 1
Leaving an end of thread to be darned in later (inside the wrapping threads) and working with three bundles of fabric threads at a time, bring the needle out at 1 and weave over (in at 2) and under (out at 3) and over (in at 4).

STEP 2
Turn the needle and work the reverse: out at 5, in at 6, out at 7, and so on.

STEP 3
When you have four binding or wrapping threads on each bundle, move over one bundle and repeat on the remaining two and the next bundle of three fabric threads.

STEP 4
Change colour and continue until the work area is filled.

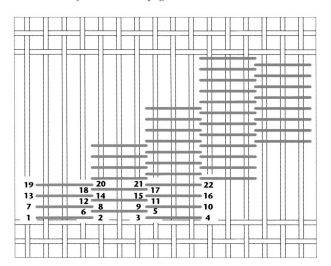

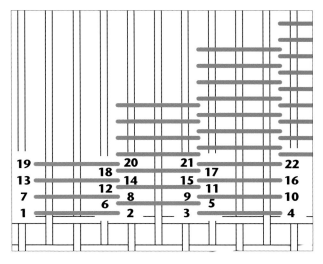

Many different patterns are possible, using one colour or several.

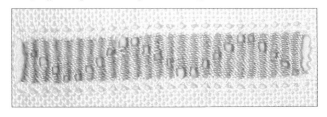

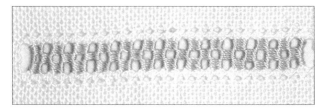

Pattern darning

A

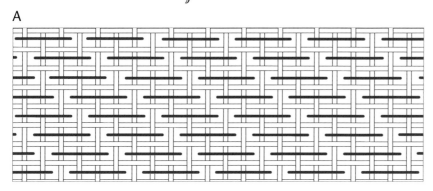

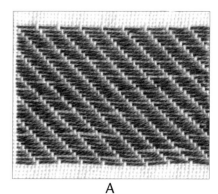

The above pattern is over three threads and under one thread. Subsequent rows are worked so that the picked-up thread advances one weft thread, giving a twill weave effect. Either A or B can be worked vertically.

B

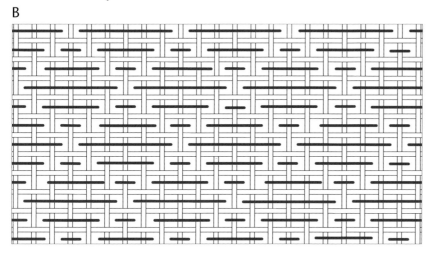

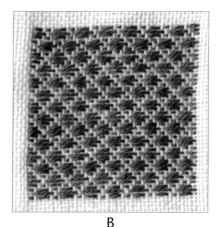

The attractive diamond pattern is suitable for a large area.

Romanian self-couching

The distinguishing feature of Romanian self-couching is that the tying or couching stitches are long and diagonal.

Other books recommend making the stitch with one long vertical stitch secured by a series of long diagonal stitches.

I find it much easier to make all the couching stitches first, then to thread the long stitch underneath the whole line. As far as I can see, the result is indistinguishable from the 'approved' way of making the stitches.

STEP 1

Working vertically, make a series of diagonal stitches: bring the needle up at 1, pass it over two threads and up six threads and insert it at 2; pass it to the left and under two threads to bring it up at 3; and so on.

STEP 2

Turn, bring the needle up at 7 and pass the thread under all the diagonal stitches, inserting it at 8.

STEP 3

Repeat for subsequent rows.

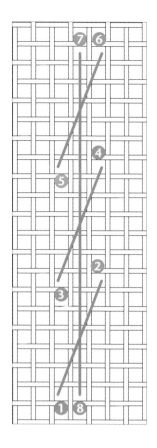

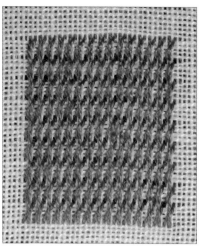

'Typical cone' motif worked in Romanian self-couching with modern threads.

Towel end worked in Romanian self-couching stitch. AUTHOR'S COLLECTION

Satin stitch

The encroaching satin stitch sample in multi-coloured thread can be used as a border or an edging as the lower row of satin stitch will secure the underside.

Straight stitches pass evenly (uncounted) from one side to the other of the area to be filled.

Satin stitch is suitable for narrow areas only, as long stitches would snag.

Two Vandyke borders in satin stitch.

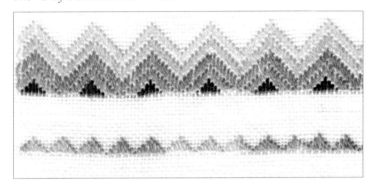

In the pink flower motif, the stems and leaves in gold thread are in satin stitch.

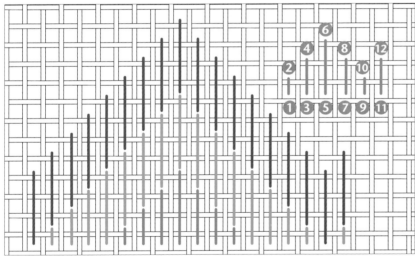

The versatility of satin stitch is shown using encroaching stitches.

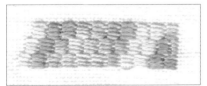

Encroaching satin stitch.

Encroaching Vandyke satin stitch.

Single-faced satin stitch

The description of single-faced satin stitch is given as the first stage of atma stitch (page 22).

The fabric for this embroidery was hand-woven on a small loom from heavy cotton or linen. The embroidery threads are heavy and aniline-dyed. The outline of the design is in pencil. It has been well used, with some mending very visible.

The piece was made to be hung folded with the two fronts visible. The short ends are finished with fine plaiting 6 cm (2 in) deep. The design is classical, with repeats of the main 'hunchback' motif. The short-edge border is simply a row of chain stitch; the side edges are sprays of flowers, coming up as deep as the main motif only.

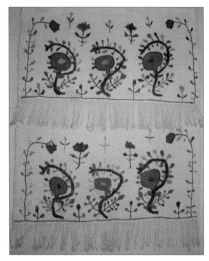

This embroidery is made up of single-faced satin stitch with some chain stitch.
PATSY ARMSTRONG COLLECTION

Turkish punch stitch

It was an exciting moment to discover two stoles, each about 62 x 200 cm (24.5 x 79 in) and weighing 300 g (10 oz), made from cotton netting and embroidered all over in Turkish punch stitch, one black with gold plate and the other cream with silver plate.

I cannot begin to describe how this was done. Each piece of plate was fixed in place separately. A Turkish travelling salesman's catalogue from the early 20th century showed samples of this work, and I understand Edna Wark explains how it was done in her book, *Drawn Fabric Embroidery*.

A section of the white and silver Turkish punch stitch stole.
PATSY ARMSTRONG COLLECTION

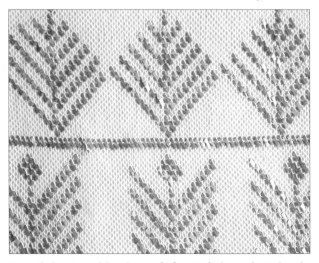

Magnified section of the white and silver Turkish punch stitch stole.

Turkish triangular stitch

This diagram looks the same as that for musabak stitch (page 32), but the method of working is quite different. In Turkish triangular stitch the diagonals are worked last and are therefore dominant. The stitches are not pulled as in musabak stitch.

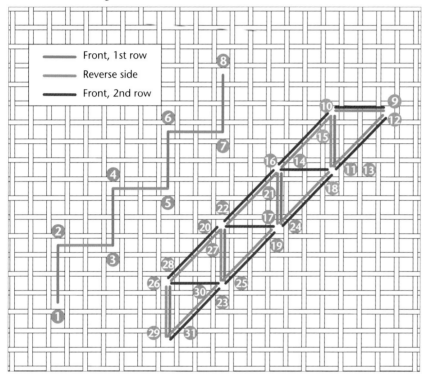

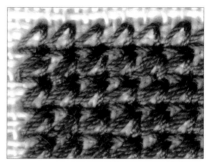

Magnification of a sample of Turkish triangular stitch worked in Mercer No. 20 crochet cotton on linen (10 threads per cm/26 threads per in).

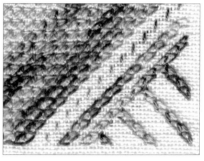

Sample of Turkish triangular stitch in No. 8 perle threads, showing the various steps and directions in which this stitch may be worked.

STEP 1

Work a row of vertical steps: bring the needle out at 1, go up three threads and insert it at 2; go under and across three threads and bring the needle out at 3; in at 4, out at 5, and so on.

STEP 2

At the top of the column of steps, take the needle three threads to the right at the back of the fabric, then bring it out at 9 on the front.

Make a horizontal stitch by passing the needle to the left across three threads and insert it into the top of the vertical stitch, at 10.

Take the needle under the vertical stitch, then bring it out at the bottom of it, at 11.

* Make a stitch on top of the fabric diagonally up to the first horizontal stitch, inserting the needle at 12.

Come back to the bottom of the last vertical stitch, bringing the needle out at 13 (same hole as 11), so that there is a diagonal stitch on both sides of the fabric.

Make a stitch horizontally by

inserting the needle at 14 at the top of the next vertical stitch.

Pass the needle behind the fabric, diagonally back to the top of the previous vertical stitch, and bring it out at 15.

Make a stitch on top of the fabric diagonally down to the top of the next vertical stitch, inserting the needle at 16 (same hole as 14).

* Take the needle under the vertical stitch, then bring it out at the bottom of it, at 17.

Make a stitch on top of the fabric diagonally up to the previous

horizontal stitch, inserting the
needle at 18.

Repeat from * to * working from
the top to the bottom of the
column.

Each stitch is made twice, once on
the front and once on the rear of
the fabric.

STEP 3
Work a new row by making a
series of vertical steps into the first
row, and repeat Step 2 to form the
diagonal stitches front and back.

Note
The central diagonal line will
be doubled.

The front must look the same
as the back.

Wave stitch

Note
By working another pair of rows offset, double-sided cross stitch can
be made.

Other shapes of stitches can be made by going up two threads and
across two threads, or up three threads and across two threads, and so
on.

By going up, say, three threads and then straight down three threads,
you create dog tooth stitch.

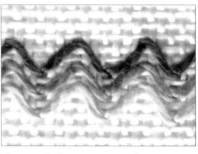

*The sample shown is a magnification in
No. 8 perle on linen (10 threads per cm/26
threads per in).*

STEP 1
Working from left to right, make a
row of diagonal stitches as shown.

Bring the needle out of the fabric
at the odd numbers and insert it at
the even numbers.

STEP 2
Return, working from right to left,
and fill in the gaps with another
row of diagonal stitches as shown.

Bring the needle out of the fabric
at the odd numbers and insert it at
the even numbers.

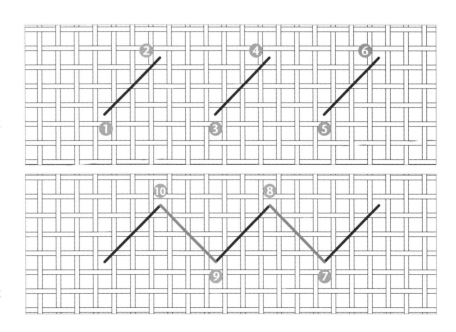

Projects

The projects are examples of how Ottoman embroidery could be used today, pictorially, or as soft furnishings or on small articles for personal use.

Table scarf, designed and stitched by Valerie Candy.

Greetings cards

A good way to practise new stitches is to make small articles like little pictures for greetings cards. Each of these can be made in a few hours.

If you want your embroidery to be seen from both sides, choose from the following stitches: satin stitch for the stems, double running stitch for the floral centre, leaves and outlining, and the uniquely Ottoman stitch, musabak, for the petals and perhaps the centre of the flower.

The design for the card shows the typical Ottoman 'lean'. The floral spray is 'wafting in the breeze'. A variety of colour schemes are illustrated here.

The design can be adapted to make circular or square coasters using commercially available acrylic mounts.

You will need

- Commercially available window card.

- A piece of closely woven cotton fabric 30 cm (12 in) square with a piece of evenweave fabric such as lugana (10 threads per cm/25 threads per in), 12 x 15 cm (5 x 6 in) machined to the middle.

  Carefully cut away the cotton fabric from behind the evenweave fabric and zigzag around the edges.

- A good, tight embroidery hoop frame.

- A blunt tapestry needle, size 24 or 26.

- Embroidery threads of your choice, including any smooth flat metallic thread that goes in a needle.

- A water-proof fine fibre-tip pen and a small piece of vilene (optional).

- Double-sided adhesive tape.

- Sewing machine and thread.

- Sequins (optional).

Ottoman embroidery is double-sided, so you can cut a rectangle from the back of the card to reveal this feature if you desire. If you do not want the reverse to show, simply affix a piece of iron-on fabric to the back of the embroidery and glue it behind the opening in the card.

Method

✂ Put the prepared fabric in a tight embroidery hoop so that the taut fabric can sit flat on a table. Use a light-box or tape the design onto a window. Centralise the frame with the fabric over the design. With a fine (0.8 mm) fibre-tip pen or similar, carefully draw the design onto the fabric.

✂ Work the design using two strands of thread in the needle at a time (except for the edges, which are worked in one strand of metallic thread).

Mounting the embroidery in the card

✂ Open the card out and put a small square of double-sided adhesive tape on the top and bottom of the inside of the rectangular opening to hold the embroidery in place during machining.

✂ Without taking the embroidery out of the frame, position the opening in the card centrally.

✂ Put the frame with the card attached under the needle of the sewing machine. It may be necessary to remove the foot temporarily.

✂ Machine along the groove around the card opening. If the corners tear, carefully stitch a sequin in each corner.

✂ Tie the machine-threads behind and cut the fabric away from the back of the card. Fold the card.

A group of cards and coasters embroidered by the author and Shirley Martin.

Elegant neckpiece

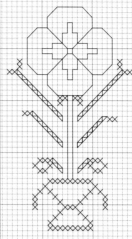

Because of its opulence and use of metallic threads, Ottoman embroidery is suitable for making small articles for personal adornment. The elegant neckpiece uses only cross stitch, double running, Turkish triangular and musabak stitches. The rose motif is easily adapted.

Method

❈ Mark the centre of your fabric.

❈ Decide on the position of the flower. Put a pencil through the centre of a cotton reel, place this on the centre line, make a dot and draw around it.

❈ Draw right-angled diagonals through the centre of the flower and make four petals.

❈ Following the graph above, satin stitch the stem over two threads. The Turkish triangular greenery, the cross stitch outline of the vase and the musabak background are also worked over two threads.

❈ The pink flower petals are worked over three threads.

❈ Outline the greenery and stems in one strand in double running and the flower in one strand in chain stitch.

❈ Cut a piece of firm cotton fabric the exact width of and slightly longer than the embroidery.

❈ Make the fringe by knotting machine-cotton firmly and running small tacking threads from the middle of the fabric to the end. Thread a bugle bead and a small pink bead onto the needle, turn and pass the needle back up the bugle. Tack into the fabric a few centimetres and fasten off securely.

❈ Continue stitching each strand of the fringe separately in a similar manner. You may need to make a small hem at the bottom of the cotton. Put it behind the embroidery, cut a piece of backing fabric and carefully slip stitch the front and back together, trapping the fringe and interlining inside.

❈ Finish the bottom by threading a line of pink beads, couching every third one onto the embroidery. Finish with a 'chain' of bugle, gold and pink beads.

You will need

☙ A piece of evenweave fabric (10 threads per cm/26 threads per in, or similar) big enough to go inside a 12 cm (5 in) embroidery frame that has had the inside ring bound with tape or binding.

☙ Pencil and cotton reel.

☙ A medium tapestry needle and a sharp needle for darning ends.

☙ Bugle beads and small, pink and gold beads for the fringe and the neck 'chain'.

☙ Mercer ecru thread for the fringe and 'chain'.

☙ A piece of firm cotton fabric for the lining and fabric for back

☙ One strand only of DMC 5282 (metallic gold). Two strands each of DMC 3712 (dark pink) for the centre and DMC 3779 (pale pink) for the petals. One strand each of DMC 725 (golden yellow) and DMC 3778 (coral pink) together for the body of the vase, which has a cross stitch outline in DMC 3842 (dark turquoise); and DMC 3347 (dark green) and DMC 3348 (light green).

Lily bookmark

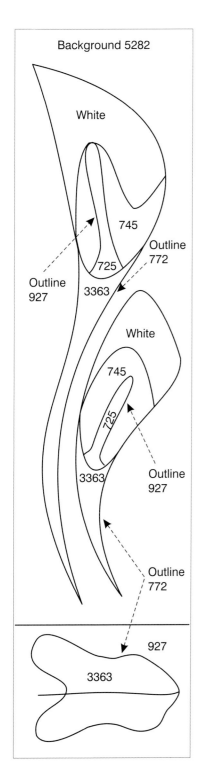

Background 5282

White

745

Outline
772

725

Outline
927

3363

White

745

725

3363

Outline
927

Outline
772

927

3363

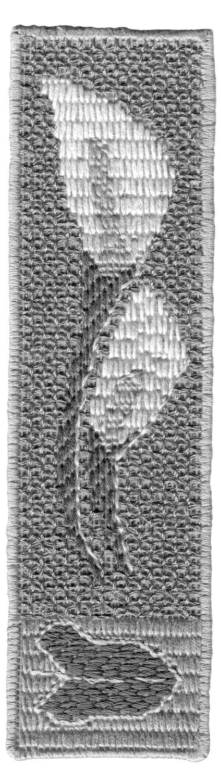

Some examples of Ottoman embroidery are similar to Assisi work in that the background is filled in, not with cross stitch, but with a pulled fabric stitch. It is difficult to pull stitches on canvas, but the unpulled murver stitch does make a very attractive canvas-work stitch. It is always a good idea to learn new stitches on a coarse fabric such as mono canvas.

The design for this bookmark was inspired by the lilies growing in my garden. The finished bookmark is 20 x 5 cm (8 x 2 in).

Preparation

✂ Frame up the canvas.

✂ Trace the design onto tissue paper or similar, and secure it face-down with adhesive tape onto the back of the stretched canvas. Turn the frame over and, using a fine fibre-tip pen, draw the design onto the canvas.

✂ Run a tacking thread around the design, leaving two threads on either side of the widest part of the design on each side. The resulting rectangle should be slightly more than 5 cm (2 in) wide and 20 cm (8 in) high.

The stitching

✂ Stitch the lilies and leaves first, but leave the outlining until all the background has been done.

✂ Using six strands of thread in the needle, stitch the leaf in dark green in diagonal orientation, leaving about 15 cm (6 in) of thread at the beginning to darn in later. Using a big-eyed needle it is possible to work with about 60 cm (24 in) of thread, even using DMC 5282. This reduces the number of ends to be darned in.

✂ Work the lilies in double running stitch in a vertical direction. Begin near the centre of each flower with the golden yellow and stitch a short distance and return. Each trip is over three and under three threads. On the return trip, make sure that you bring the needle up each time on the same side of the preceding thread to make a smooth line (refer to the dictionary of stitches).

✂ Stitch the background in DMC 5282 (metallic gold), using murver stitch (best worked up two warp threads and over four weft threads).

The finishing

✂ Turn the edges of the canvas under. With six strands of DMC 725 (golden yellow), satin stitch a border two threads deep all around the bookmark.

✂ Either line the bookmark with iron-on vilene or leave it as is. (Although murver stitch is not double-sided, it is quite pleasing on the reverse.)

✂ When ironing, always place the embroidery face-down and use a piece of baking paper between the iron and the embroidery when you use metallic threads.

You will need

༄ A piece of yellow mono interlocking canvas (6 threads per cm/14 threads per in), 25 x 15 cm (10 x 6 in) framed up.

༄ Tissue paper or similar and adhesive tape.

༄ A large tapestry needle and a fibre-tip pen.

༄ Threads for the flowers (use all six strands in the needle): DMC 3363 (dark green) and DMC 772 (light green) for the leaves and stems; DMC white for the spathes; DMC 745 (lemon) for the flower; DMC 725 (golden yellow) for the centre; three strands of DMC 927 (blue grey) for the leaf background and outlines; all of these threads are worked in double running stitch.

༄ Thread for the background: DMC perle No. 5 5282 (metallic gold), done in murver stitch (take care not to split the stitches).

༄ Thread for the satin stitch edging: DMC 725 (golden yellow), six strands.

༄ Vilene (optional).

Canvas-work sampler — the Ottoman rose

Although the design for this sampler is original, it is based on Ottoman tile patterns and embodies a number of textiles that I studied. In this one piece, many of the stitches of the 17th, 18th and 19th centuries are represented. The large flower and the surrounding gold pattern darning are 17th century, while the rosebuds and the background in the lower part are stitches that were common from the 18th century. The 'tulip' petal, stitched in double running, and the 'branches' petal, stitched in pattern darning, are typical of 17th-century embroideries, and in fine cotton fabric (19 threads per cm/48 threads per in) were left void. Outlines were stitched in brown, black, rust or any other colour (not gold) at that time. The designs were abstract floral in bright primaries and green. Later the designs became more realistic and pastel in palette, with extensive use of precious metal wire wound on silk threads of various colours.

'Ottoman rose' was a colour popular in the 19th century as a house paint.

You will need

- ❧ A piece of mono canvas (6 threads per cm/14 threads per in), 30 x 45 cm (12 x 18 in) framed up.

- ❧ A narrow strip of cotton fabric and a stapler.

- ❧ A fine felt-tip pen.

- ❧ Two tapestry needles, one large and one small, and a sharp needle for darning in the ends.

- ❧ One hank each of the following DMC perle threads:

  DMC perle No. 3:

  3046 (dull gold) for the background pattern darning.

  3328 (deep pink) for the central floral trefoil.

  White/blanc for the four petals.

  DMC perle No. 5:

  3046 (dull gold) for the musabak and murver background areas, the diagonal areas in half cross stitch between the white petals and the 'tulip' and 'branches' inside the two horizontal petals.

  3813 (pale blue/green) for the couching on the atma stitch flower centre.

  3813 and 502 (pale and mid blue/green) for the stem, leaves and calyxs in half cross stitch.

- ❧ A small quantity of unspun silk or heavy viscose thread in white or pale green for the atma stitch centre.

- ❧ DMC stranded cotton 5282 (metallic gold) for the outlines of the buds, stem, leaves and calyxs, the 'tulip' and the 'branches'.

- ❧ One strand of DMC 5282 is used in the needle with DMC No. 3 white/blanc in the petals that are worked in Turkish triangular stitch and Bukhara couching.

Sampler designed by the author and stitched by Shirley Martin.

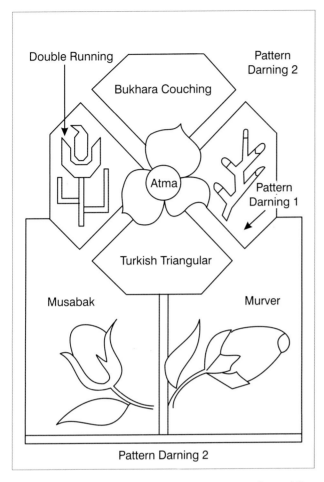

Double Running

Bukhara Couching

Pattern Darning 2

Atma

Pattern Darning 1

Turkish Triangular

Musabak

Murver

Pattern Darning 2

This pattern has been reduced to fit the page. To reproduce it full size, enlarge it to 200% on a photocopier.

Preparation of the canvas

Either frame up a piece of mono canvas (6 threads per cm/14 threads per in) about 30 x 45 cm (12 x 18 in) on a tapestry frame in the traditional manner; or using a frame of 2.5 cm (1 in) square dressed pine, about 28 x 42 cm (11 x 16.5 in), staple the canvas in place.

Always put a narrow strip of cotton fabric over the mono canvas before you staple — this is to avoid damaging the canvas when you remove the staples; make sure the canvas is taut; staple the four centres first, then, with uniform tension on the canvas, staple securely in place.

Fasten a copy of the design to the underside of the canvas and trace it with a fine felt-tip pen.

Method

If you find the coloured canvas difficult to see, work with a big sheet of plain white paper on the table beneath the canvas. If convenient, screw the working frame to an upright stand, or work with one end on a table.

To work the background

✄ Start the background at the top-centre of the large flower, using DMC perle No. 3 3046 (gold). Use pattern darning stitch as described in the dictionary of stitches.

✄ Leaving a tail to be darned in later, commence with a long vertical stitch over five threads. Pick up one thread, pass over five, pick up one, pass over five, and so on, finishing at the top with a long stitch that passes over five threads.

✄ Turn, and return under one thread, over three, under one, over one, and repeat until you reach the flower.

✄ Turn, and return over one thread, under one, over one, under one, over three, under one, and so on to the top border.

✄ Continue until you have the same number of patterns on either side of the centre.

✄ The diamond pattern darning area comes down the sides of the flower and along the bottom as shown in the picture.

48

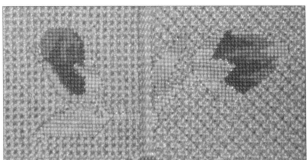

To work the flowers

✄ Work the four petals of the main flower, excluding the 'tulip' and the 'branches', in DMC perle No. 3 white/blanc, using the stitches as indicated in the pattern opposite.

✄ Fill in the 'tulip' and the 'branches' with DMC perle No. 5 3046 (dull gold) in half cross stitch.

✄ Work the diagonals between the petals in DMC perle No. 5 3046 in half cross stitch.

✄ Work the 'trefoil' in DMC perle No. 3 3328 (deep pink) in musabak stitch.

✄ Work the centre of the flower in atma stitch using unspun silk or heavy viscose thread in single-faced satin stitch secured by Bukhara couching in DMC perle No. 5 3813 (pale blue/green).

✄ Work the 'rosebuds' and leaves according to the picture in half cross stitch.

✄ Work the stem in vertical rows of double running stitch, one row in DMC perle No. 5 3813 (pale blue/green), one row in DMC perle 502 (medium blue/green), and one row of DMC stranded cotton 5282 (metallic gold).

To work the lower backgrounds

✄ Using DMC perle No. 5 3046 (gold), stitch the lower backgrounds in musabak and murver stitches as indicated.

To finish

✄ Use satin stitch over two threads to finish around the perimeter neatly, also 12 threads up from the bottom, and two-thirds of the way down the flower as shown.

✄ When complete, press your embroidery on the wrong side with a piece of baking paper between the embroidery and the iron.

✄ Mount or frame as preferred. Shirley Martin mounted her embroidery on a stretcher frame and added a box frame covered in dull gold Thai silk.

*N*ote
The musabak stitch is worked over three threads of canvas and the murver stitch is worked across four weft and up two warp threads of canvas.

Lily cushion

The earliest Ottoman embroideries were made in simple pattern darning so that most of the precious silk thread was on the visible surface. The inspiration for the design of this cushion was calla lilies grown in our garden. Although the Ottoman patterns were generally more flowing, this is good as a learning piece, and careful manipulation of commercially available variegated threads makes for economy of materials — always a consideration now as then!

My original embroidery was called 'Trinity'. It was 'painted' with a jumble of outdated and unnumbered stranded threads that cluttered one of my sewing boxes. I used double running stitch, typical of the Ottoman Rococo period, to demonstrate its effectiveness as a realistic filling stitch.

The design for the cushion was counted from the graph.

You will need

- A piece of ivory Cork linen (7 threads per cm/19 threads per in), about 50 cm (20 in) square; be sure to zigzag the edges as this fabric frays.

- Firm furnishing fabric the same colour as the Cork linen for the backing, 50 x 70 cm (20 x 27.5 in).

- A tapestry needle for the stitchery and a sharp needle for darning in ends.

- Anchor multi-colour perle No. 5 1315 (red–yellow) and Anchor multi-colour perle No. 5 1305 (yellow–apricot–gold) for the spathes.

- Anchor perle No. 5 1355 (blue–lime–green) for the leaves.

- Some DMC perle No. 5 725 (golden yellow) and DMC perle No. 5 782 (old gold) for details in the spathes.

- DMC perle No. 8 920 (rust) for all the outlining.

- Yellow, orange, red and green oddments of embroidery stranded cotton or floss left over from other projects for the tassels, which have DMC perle No. 5 725 (golden yellow) tie ends and detached buttonhole stitch heads.

- A piece of firm card 24 x 16 cm (9 x 6 in).

- Two 2.5 cm (1 in) buttons for the back of the cushion, and a cushion pad 40 cm (16 in) square.

- A fine, waterproof fibre-tip pen.

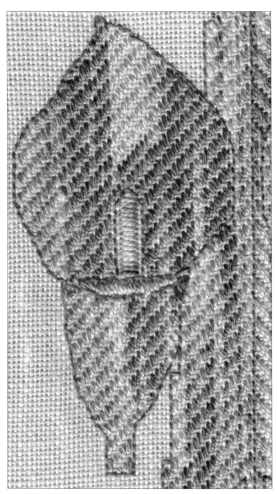

Legend: *Golden yellow central portion of spathe —*
DMC perle No. 5 725; dull-gold streaks — DMC perle
No. 5 782; variegated yellow-sided spathe — Anchor
multi-colour perle No. 5 1305; orange red — Anchor
multi-colour perle No. 5 1315; variegated green centre
and leaf — Anchor multi-colour perle No. 5 1355.

*N*ote
Each square of the graph represents two
warp and two weft threads.

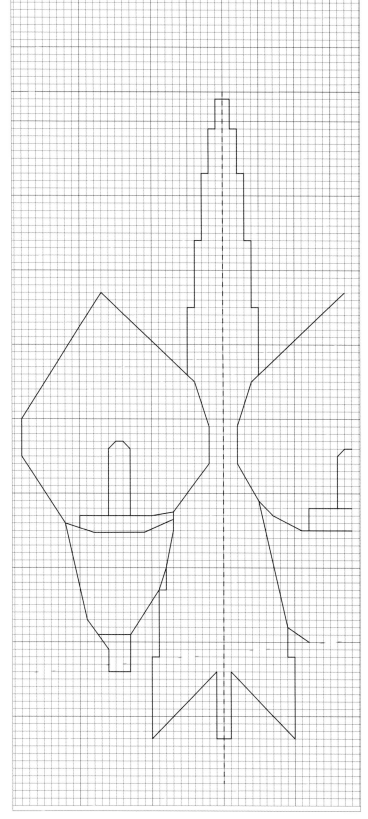

Preparation

✂ Mark the horizontal and vertical central lines of your fabric by tacking with a blue sewing thread.

✂ Tack up the central line of each flower, and tack a line across the tops of the pistils. These are useful guidelines which are removed as you work.

✂ Trace the design (as given on page 51) onto the linen using a fine, waterproof fibre-tipped pen and a light-box — take care that your verticals really are vertical!

✂ Using DMC No. 8 920 (rust), stitch the outline using double running stitch, starting at the raised central flower stalk. Work over two and under two fabric threads, noting that sometimes you will need to work over two and up three threads, for instance, in order to get a smooth curve. Hint: when outlining a design I always work only the first 'journey' of the double running stitch, leaving the second 'journey' (the return line of stitches) until the end to neaten the filling stitches.

To stitch the flowers

✂ Using the photograph of the finished cushion and the coloured drawing of the lilies, fill in the spathes and the leaves in pattern darning. Use the threads described above and work vertically, always up

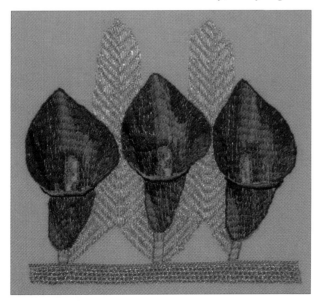

three and under one thread. The pattern darning is worked in the diagonal orientation — the next row is stitched so that the next 'under' thread is one thread above the previous row.

✂ Discard sections of the multi-coloured thread if you wish, but keep the pieces for the tassels.

To make the tassels

✂ Bend a firm piece of card roughly 24 x 16 cm (9 x 6 in) in half lengthwise.

✂ Using your ends of multi-coloured perle and any other scraps of embroidery floss, wind all four tassels on the same piece of card, making sure they are all the same thickness.

✂ Making one tassel at a time, thread a tapestry needle with DMC perle No. 5 725 (golden yellow) and run it under the folded end of the card. Tie firmly before cutting the bottom of the tassel.

✂ Wind the perle firmly around the top of the tassel, hiding your end thread in the skirt.

✂ With a new thread, cover the head with a cap of detached buttonhole stitch (see the dictionary of stitches, page 25).

To make up the cushion

✂ Cut the backing piece in half and make two equally spaced buttonholes.

✂ Do up the buttons and stitch the ends to make a piece of fabric the same size as the embroidered front.

✂ Machine the two pieces together and turn right-side out.

✂ Secure a tassel at each corner by threading the two yellow perle No. 5 ends into a tapestry needle, pushing them into the cushion and stitching them firmly into the seam allowance before tying off.

'Trinity'. On The finer fabric, the base, stems, pistils and leaves were counted and the lilies traced using a light box.

Three coasters

This set of three coasters was designed to show the major stitches used over the four centuries of Ottoman embroidery that I studied. Many of the early stitches were used right through to the 19th century.

Embroideries from the 17th century were done in strong, clear primary colours, with green and often brown or black for the borders of the individual motifs. After the 18th century, examples show extensive use of metallic threads and soft pastel colours. Very little purple is seen until the advent of the aniline dyes in the late 19th century. In the late 19th century we also see the use of gold-coloured plate or strips. Sometimes this plate was copper washed with silver, and therefore what we see today is the tarnished metal. This set of coasters uses colours compatible with those used at the time, but colours to fit any decor could be used.

The design for the 17th-century coaster was devised by cutting up a circle of paper into pleasing shapes, discarding some where necessary. It is not, therefore, a typical Ottoman pattern, but it is an abstracted plant form such as you might find in a mirror cover of the era. The 18th-century coaster was inspired by a motif in an 18th-century yaglik and is more realistically floral, as is the design for the 19th-century coaster. Animals and birds featured occasionally in domestic

A finished coaster, with Turkish coffee cups and saucers.

embroidery prior to the early 1900s.

It is quite common to find large spaces, such as leaves, filled in with sprays of flowers, little tulips, small knobs or seeds. You can see why when faced with the task of filling in big spaces with boring pattern darning. Seemingly pointless blobs and shapes often appear in embroideries of this era — it's a quick and easy way of balancing up a design. They can also be seen on hand-painted porcelain. Another way of balancing a design is with colour: bright strong colours appear to have more weight than pale delicate ones.

You will need

- A piece of evenweave fabric 10 threads per cm/26 threads per in, or 11 threads per cm/29 threads per in, about 25 cm (10 in) square for each coaster. Begin by tracing the pictures of each, using a light-box and a waterproof fibre-tip pen.

Note

Draw your patterns centrally on the fabric.

Choose your colour scheme from the suggestions given.

The finished designs might simply be hemmed to make cocktail coasters, or framed as a set of little pictures.

Presentation in elaborate little gold frames accentuates the precious nature of the planet's plant life, and also echoes the Byzantine influence of the area around Istanbul.

Colour scheme:

Terracotta, medium coral pink, medium and deep slate blue, and golden yellow. DMC stranded cotton 995 (turquoise) outlines the Romanian couching cusp (one strand only) and the pattern darning stitch leaf (two strands).

Atma circle (yellow)

- Single-faced satin stitch in Anchor Marlitt 1078 (gold), 4 strands.

- Bukhara self-couching in DMC perle No. 8 726 (golden yellow) for the laid threads over every third weft thread of the fabric.

- Chain stitch edge to the circle in DMC perle No. 8 726 (golden yellow).

Romanian self-couching cusp (medium slate blue)

- DMC No. 8 perle 932 (medium slate blue); the tying or couching stitches are worked diagonally over one and up four warp threads.

Turkish triangular stitch shape (coral pink)

- Three strands of DMC stranded cotton 3778 (coral pink), worked over three warp and three weft threads.

Pattern darning shape (terracotta)

- Three strands of DMC stranded cotton 3830 (terracotta), worked vertically over five and under one thread.

Pattern darning leaf shape (deep slate blue)

- DMC perle No. 8 930 (slate blue), worked horizontally over five and under one thread; the little bobbles are in two strands of DMC stranded cotton 725 (golden yellow).

Alternative colour scheme:

Turquoise, red, yellow, cream and green, slate blue.

Atma circle DMC perle No. 5 3078 (cream) over Anchor Marlitt 1036.

Turkish triangular shape DMC perle No. 5 309 (red).

Romanian self-couching cusp DMC perle No. 5 726 (golden yellow).

Pattern darning shape DMC perle No. 5 995 (turquoise).

Pattern darning shape with leaf DMC perle No. 5 930 (slate blue), red bobbles, outline in DMC perle No. 5 469 (green).

Note

Either of these motifs could be repeated three or four times along each end of a table scarf.

An 18th-century poppy coaster

Colour scheme:
Turquoise, dull gold and soft neutrals.

Small oval leaf in double running stitch DMC 739 (cream).

Sepals in double running stitch DMC 407 (dull pink).

Bud and poppy in murver stitch DMC 995 (turquoise).

'Oak leaves' in musabak stitch DMC 372 (gold beige) or DMC 3013 (pale green).

Other leaves in musabak stitch DMC 3013 (pale green).

Smallest leaf in double running stitch DMC 995 (turquoise).

Outlines are in double running stitch DMC perle No. 5 5282 (metallic gold).

A 19th-century lily and rosebud coaster

Two threads of DMC stranded cotton are used throughout. The lily and the rosebuds are in musabak stitch; the stems, sepals, leaves, little blue florets and the outlining are in double running.

Colour scheme:
Three pinks in the lily; lemon bud; blue florets; green stems; gold edges.

Lily petals DMC 3779 (pale pink), DMC 352 (mid pink), DMC 3712 (dark pink).

Rosebuds DMC 3779 (pale pink) and DMC 745 (lemon).

Florets DMC 3753 (light slate blue).

Leaves, etc. DMC 3013 (pale green).

Outlines DMC perle No. 5 5282 (metallic gold), split in half; use no more than 30 cm (12 in) lengths in the needle as the thread frays easily.

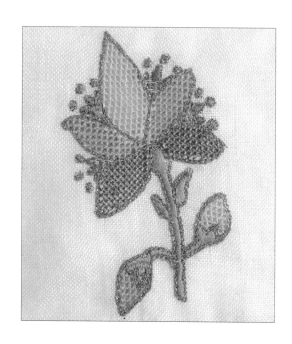

Collection of Ottoman borders and motifs

The purpose of this project is to introduce some of the very attractive border patterns used in 18th- and 19th-century Ottoman embroideries, and to practise some of the stitches that are unique to that art form. In this project, each square on all graphs represents two warp and two weft threads of fabric.

In five years of reading and studying Ottoman embroidery I have seen only three photographs of samplers, and in each the borders and motifs were quite randomly arranged. In other words, they were 'spot samplers', made as memory guides. There are also examples of work done in mercerized cotton and cheap tinsel instead of silk and gold or silver gilt (perhaps the work of children or apprentices) and these are inferior examples of typical yagliks. Unlike many English samplers, neither the maker's name nor the date of completion appears on the samplers. Sometimes markings in Indian ink occur on embroideries and these are thought to be either workshop markings or indications of ownership, as embroideries were often pooled for special occasions, such as weddings and circumcisions.

Ottoman embroiderers would have drawn their motifs directly onto the narrow-loomed fabric, whereas the designs in this section are graphed. Sometimes I find it convenient to count geometrical areas, like vases, bowls and vertical stems of flower sprays, and to trace the curvilinear parts. All the designs have been adapted from pictures, cards and personal drawings of Ottoman embroideries that I have studied.

Stitches used

Refer to the dictionary of stitches.

Detached buttonhole stitch edge
Ottoman hemstitching
Needleweaving border
Double running
Musabak
Murver
Double saw tooth
Turkish triangular
Satin
Chain
Wave
Cross stitches

You will need

- A piece of antique white or similar-coloured fabric, 10 threads per cm/26 threads per in, approximately 40 x 25 cm (16 x 10 in).

- One or two hanks of DMC stranded thread 5282 (metallic gold).

- DMC stranded threads in the following colours: 746 (cream), 3712 (dark pink), 3779 (pale pink), 3052 (pale green), 367 (mid green), 3363 (dark green), 935 (very dark green), 725 (golden yellow), 927 (blue grey), 3843 (turquoise).

- The detached buttonhole stitch edge and the crochet lace edging are worked in cream perle or metallic thread. (Instructions for crochet are not included.)

- A medium-sized tapestry needle, with not too small an eye, and a sharp needle for darning in ends. A piece of beeswax would be useful.

- An embroidery hoop, the inside ring bound with tape or bias binding.

- Coloured machine-thread for tacking the design layout.

- A reel of cream machine-thread for finishing the edges.

Collection of Ottoman borders and motifs.

Preparing the fabric

❋ Zigzag around the whole of the fabric in a matching thread.

❋ Run a tacking thread vertically to mark the centre of the fabric in a contrasting machine-thread.

❋ Create a tacking line 2 cm (0.75 in) up from the bottom: beginning at the centre and stitching first in one direction and then in the other, tack in contrasting machine-thread over three threads and under three threads so that you have equal multiples of nine threads on either side; this should bring you to about 2 cm (0.75 in) from each side.

❋ In the centre, just above the 2 cm (0.75 in) tacking line, carefully cut a thread; count the warp threads and withdraw in multiples of nine to approximately 2 cm (0.75 in) from the long edges on either side; above it, cut and draw out six more weft threads. You now have a rectangle of warp threads only with a fringe at either side.

❋ Either darn back the withdrawn ends on the wrong side of the fabric, ending the darned portion at a different place each time, and cut off the ends; or nip off the withdrawn threads and, with fine sewing thread, stitch over the end several times; this will not show if the hemstitching extends to cover it.

❋ Eight threads above the framed rectangle, run a line of tacking over four and under four threads; start at the centre and work outwards.

❋ Further rows of tacking will be needed as you progress.

A sample of motifs that can be adapted for a number of projects. These are details from a collar by the author.

Needleweaving border

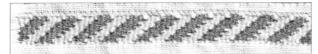

❋ First work Ottoman hemstitching along the long sides of the rectangle of drawn threads, working over three and down three threads to form bundles of warp threads that should be a multiple of nine. Use your tacking as a guide.

❋ Following the instructions for needleweaving as given for the bottom pattern in the dictionary of stitches (page 33), thread the needle with one strand of DMC 5282 metallic thread. Use 60 cm (24 in) lengths in a medium-sized needle (so that the eye will not rub and fray the thread). The whole process is easier if the thread is pulled through beeswax before stitching begins.

❋ To begin, make a few running stitches on the fabric (these will be darned in later). Weave the needle in and out over three bundles of warp threads four times.

❋ Move one bundle over and weave over two of the original bundles and the next one to it four times.

❋ Repeat until the top is reached. Darn the ends into the wrapping and change colour. Repeat to the end.

Half saw tooth border

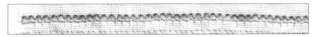

❋ With two strands of DMC 927 (blue grey) in the needle, work half of the double saw tooth stitch border (see the dictionary of stitches, page 27) over four and up four threads.

❋ Run a row of tacking six threads up from the top of the half saw tooth border.

❋ Run a vertical line of tacking up through the centre to the top of the fabric.

Rosebud motifs

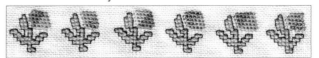

❋ The pattern for the rosebud sprigs is given below. The stems and leaves are worked in cross stitch and the outlines are in double running stitch, two strands. The rosebuds are in musabak stitch.

❋ Start with the central rosebud by making the first cross of the stem at the base of the motif on the central tacking line. There are 23 threads between motifs.

Colour scheme

Stems and leaves

❋ DMC 3052 (pale green), two strands; outlines in DMC 935 (very dark green), one strand.

Rosebuds

❋ DMC 3779 (pale pink), DMC 3712 (dark pink), DMC 5282 (metallic gold), all with two strands in the needle; it is interesting to use slightly different pinks but make sure they are of the same intensity.

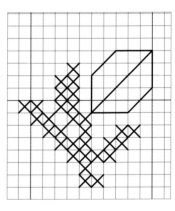

Another border of half saw tooth stitch

Eight threads above the top of the rosebuds work a line of half saw tooth stitch in one strand of DMC 927 (blue grey) over four and up four threads.

Murver stitch border

Three threads above the second half saw tooth stitch border, work a band of murver stitch in DMC 5282 (metallic gold), one strand only; stitch up three and across six threads and make the band 21 threads deep.

Vandyke satin stitch border

✤ Leaving a row one thread deep above the murver stitch border, make a line of Vandykes working over five threads, using two strands of DMC stranded cottons in the colours that you are using in the other borders and motifs, such as 927 (blue grey), 3779 (pale pink), 3052 (pale green), 367 (mid green), and 725 (golden yellow).

✤ Tack a horizontal line right across the fabric three threads above the top of the Vandykes.

Three flowers border

This motif of a single flower rising from a small vase, or a bouquet of blooms flowing out of a minute urn, occurs often and is the Ottoman version of the 'tree of life' pattern.

✤ Stitch the central motif as described for the elegant neckpiece project (page 43).

✤ From the centre of the urn, tack vertical lines 60 threads on either side. Tack horizontal lines in both directions across the top of the urn, under each set of leaves and under the flower.

✤ Complete the other two motifs.

✤ Outline the foliage on the central motif with one thread of metallic gold and the other motifs in dark green double running stitch.

✤ Edge the flower petals and centres in chain stitch in one strand of metallic gold.

✤ Outline the urn in one thread of gold double running stitch.

Hexagon ribbon border

✤ Four threads above the top of the three flowers, stitch two rows of wave stitch over four and across four threads. Work two rows, the first in gold and the second in DMC 3779 (pale pink).

✤ Starting at the middle, work the hexagon ribbon pattern (as shown below) in double running stitch in two threads of DMC 5282 (metallic gold); the centre circles are in pairs, chain stitched in DMC 3843 (turquoise) and DMC 3779 (pale pink), with tiny chain stitched centres.

✤ Complete with another two rows of wave stitch as shown.

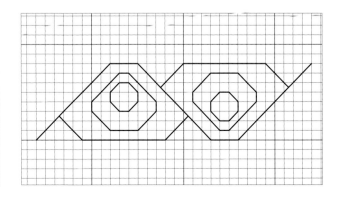

Rose and carnation motif

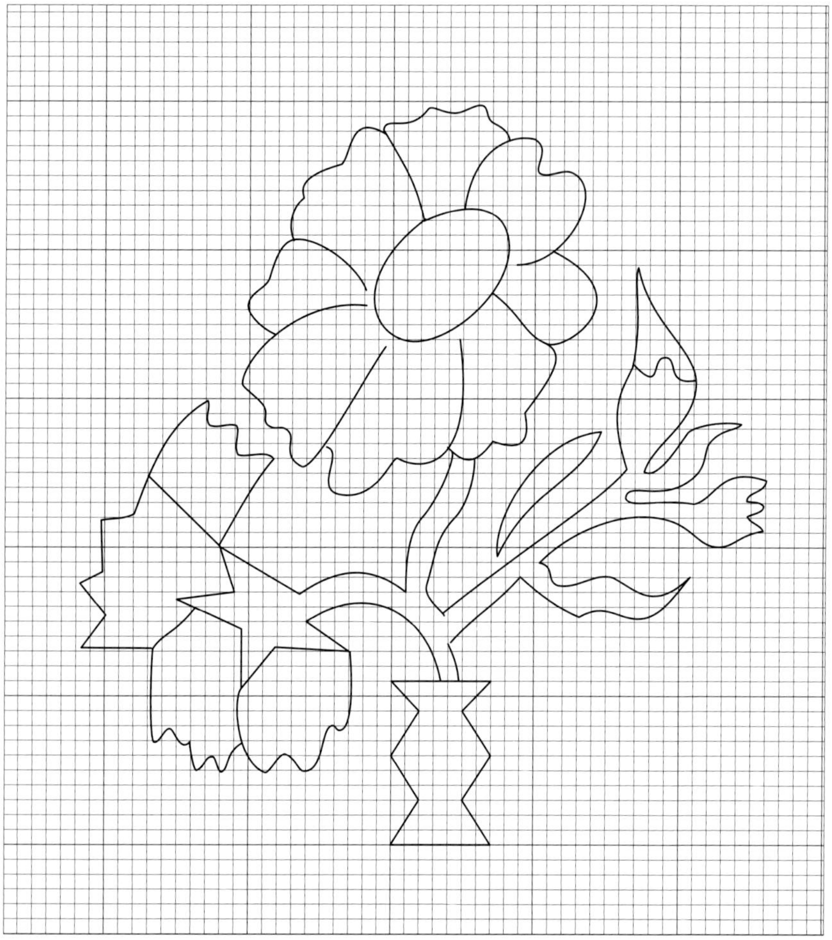

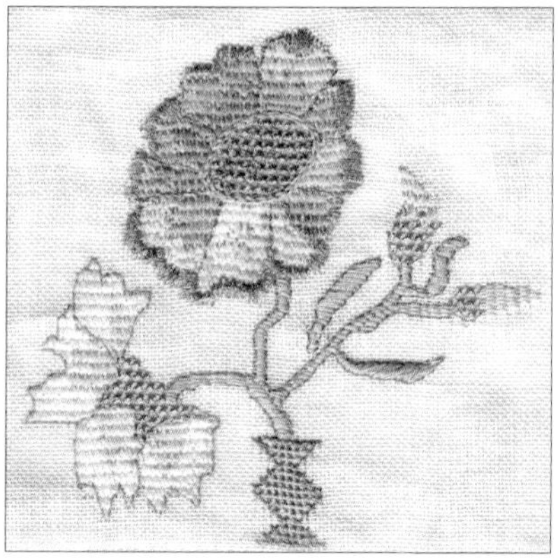

Images of carnations were found in early embroideries, usually stitched in red and white in double running stitch or pattern darning stitch. They continued to be highly favoured throughout the 18th and 19th centuries. The flowers became less formal, and we sometimes even see petals on the point of falling. Shading was introduced, and the filling was double running stitch in the soft pinks that complemented the glowing metal thread stitchery. The rows of double running stitches curved to give a realistic effect. Likewise, the rose has always been a favourite flower. In the earliest embroideries, roses were single and often yellow and red. Later they became more realistic.

- Count the vase, making sure it is centrally placed. Then either count the floral spray, outlining with machine thread in running stitch to be picked out as the work progresses. Or trace using a lightbox.
- Outline the urn in one strand of metallic gold cross stitch. The inside is musabak stitch in one strand of DMC 927 (blue grey).
- The stems are double running and satin stitches in DMC 3052 (pale green), outlined with DMC 935 (very dark green).
- The centre of the rose and the sepals of the

carnation and buds are musabak stitch over three threads in one strand of DMC 5282 (metallic gold).

❋ The buds are worked in double running stitch in two strands of DMC 725 (golden yellow).

❋ The carnation is worked in double running stitch in two strands of DMC 746 (cream) and DMC 3779 (pale pink), and outlined in double running stitch in one strand of DMC 3712 (dark pink).

❋ The rose is worked using all the pink colours from in this piece, shading with the deepest colour near the centre which is edged with two strands of chain stitch in DMC 927 (blue grey). Some white double running stitch may be added for extra interest.

❋ The outline of the rose is in satin stitch in two strands of DMC 5282 (metallic gold).

❋ The petals are separated by a line of double running stitch in DMC 5282 (metallic gold).

Another suitable motif would be the 'three pears'

The three pears

shown below. The pink, blue and lemon colours with which the original was worked are muted versions of the strong bold primary colours of an earlier era of Ottoman embroidery. This style of embroidery was a forerunner of the Art Deco style of the 1920s.

The 'three pears' motif would be very effective on table linen, and remarkably modern. The 19th-century yaglik from which this design evolved had three bowls along each end, the central one having pink pears with blue and lemon leaves sitting on a bowl of gold and two shades of lemon. Those flanking it had identical bowls with blue pears and pink and lemon leaves.

Finishing the collection of borders and motifs

In each of these examples, a thread is drawn about a centimetre from the cut edge of the fabric. This centimetre is turned to the back and a fine line of tacking is made to hold the edge down. In picture A a line of buttonhole stitch three threads between stitches is made first, and into this the crochet is worked. In B the two rows of encroaching satin stitch are worked through two layers of fabric. In C the edge is first finished with a row of buttonhole stitch, down two and across two threads, and, two threads below that, four rows of four-sided step stitch are made to hold both layers of fabric together.

In some historic examples, metal thread crochet appears but the only coloured edges I saw were in bright purple or cerise — obviously aniline dye colours — and therefore late 19th or early 20th century. Sometimes bright little bobbles were used in earlier examples.

Picot edge

- Draw a thread all round, about 10 threads from the edge. Fold at this line, slicing a little off the corners. Turn under and hem.
- On the right side, using perle No. 8 in cream or ecru, blanket stitch around the perimeter, three threads down and three threads across each stitch.
- Stitch once more around the perimeter, making four buttonhole stitches into each loop.

Other ways of finishing the piece

- Fray the short ends edging with Ottoman hemstitching and hem the long ends.
- Crochet the short ends in metallic thread and hem the long ends.

A

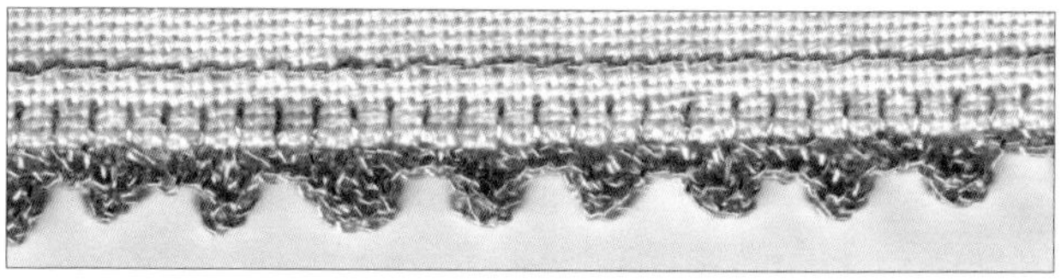

Crochet edge using metal thread with a line of double running stitch.

B

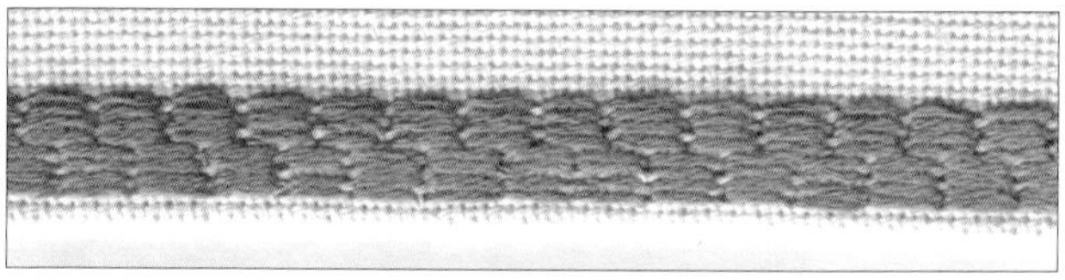

Encroaching satin stitch in pink silk thread.

C

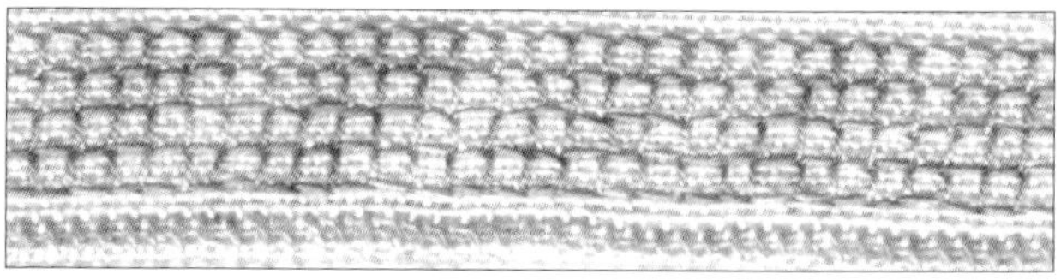

Buttonhole stitch edge with four rows of four-sided step stitch in hand-dyed thread.

More inspiration

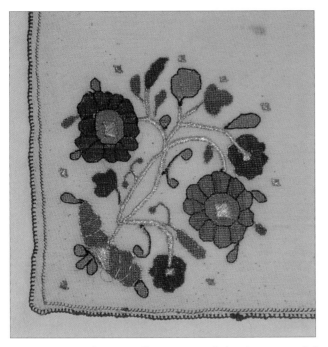 

These are corners from two silk organza tea cloths, showing simple buttonhole stitch edges. These 20th-century motifs would make charming coasters. MARGARET BOYCE COLLECTION

A 20th-century yaglik. MARGERY BLACKMAN COLLECTION

The creative leap — the Cappadocia collar

Of necessity, all of the examples in this book are interpretations. Identical fabrics and threads are not readily available today, nor do we want to make the same articles that Ottoman embroiderers needed. Our lifestyles are totally different. However, this study has taught me so much about design and observation, and has given me a great admiration of the skill of generations of embroiderers and designers from a culture quite different to mine.

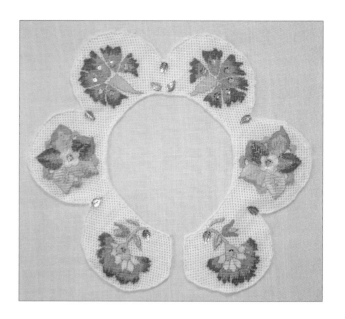

You will need

- A piece of antique white evenweave linen 26 threads per inch (10 threads per cm) 40 x 50 cm (16 x 20 in).

- Madeira Silks — three pinks, 0703 L12; 0701 L11; 06113 L11: two strands of each in the needle at a time.

- Mulberry Silk 558 (pale green) and Mulberry Silk 545 (blue/grey).

- A few centimetres of Zwicky Silk iris turquoise.

- Madeira decora (rayon) 1484 (ivory), one strand.

- Anchor Marlitt (rayon) 1013 (lemon).

- DMC perle 5282 (metallic gold), each length split in half.

- Metallic Madeira 300 machine thread.

- Mercer crochet cotton No. 60.

- Gold sequins and gold leaves.

The inclusion of rayon threads gave a lustre and sparkle to the work, as did the sequins and little gold leaves that were added last.

How the design came about

We know from past experience that often all we need to get going is to do something and the creative juices will begin to flow. When searching for inspiration for a project, and all sources have forsaken you, it's time to play a game. This is a variation of a technique taught by a visiting tutor from USA.

It consists of four sets of cards, written in different coloured felt-tip pens. The categories are 'outline', 'composition' (or 'theme'), 'colour', 'texture' — the four cornerstones of good design.

The 'outline' set of cards might include the following: an irregular shape; a shape derived from a plant; a rectangle, or any other geometric shape such as a triangle; a diamond within a circle; and so on.

The 'composition' or 'theme' set might include: a pattern organised on a grid, or a checker board; a wiggly design; one inspired by a window or a door or a manhole cover; a design cut from folded paper; one derived from a paper collage; and so on.

The 'colour' set could include colours inspired by: a rock; the sky; the sea; a mixture of black and white; 90 per cent 'warm' colours and 10 per cent 'cold' colours, or vice versa; a complementary colour scheme; an analogous colour scheme; rich jewel colours; pastel colours; and so on.

The 'texture' set could include the whole encyclopedia of stitches that embroiderers have at their disposal, as well as items such as: the texture of hair, or fur; rough or smooth; silky; woolly; crinkled; based on a textile repair.

Every time you think of an unusual colour scheme, a design source, or learn a new technique, make another card.

Just browsing through your cards might give you inspiration. Otherwise, take one from each pile at random and work on the set you get. Rejection or replacement of any or all of the cards is quite acceptable.

This is what I did when I wanted to create my collar. I played The Game. My four sets of cards were spread out in separate areas on the table and one card was drawn from each pile. The four cards I drew out were:

- Texture — based on a textile repair; darning, pattern darning, double running stitch, Ottoman embroidery.

- Colour — mainly pastel with metallic threads, more recent Ottoman embroidery.

- Composition — based on a plant; floral.

- Outline — wavy; that white chrocheted collar I bought from a girl sitting by the road on Cappadocia. The collar was lacy like the landscape.

Aided by the photographs I had taken, I remembered the blue chicory and pink geraniums with grey green leaves, little patches of grape vines fringed with straw-dry grasses, and the fruit that had been harvested, drying on blue plastic sheets in the warm autumn sun.

The Cappadocia Collar had to have an outline like the one I purchased. The pattern had to be floral, the colouring like the weeds growing around the little vineyards. The background had to be full of holes, similar to the cone-like hills of Cappadocia pockmarked with dwelling places. The stitchery had to be double running stitch for the pastel flowers and musabak stitch for the background. That was my 10 per cent inspiration.

Then came the 90 per cent perspiration required to give birth to the finished design. Suffice it is to say that it took several weeks of my spare time, a very messy workroom, half a roll of tracing paper, and lots of scrappy meals!

Completing the design

The outline of the collar had to be arranged to sit well on the neck as embroidery is less fluid than crochet.

The outline was constructed on paper using a compass. The neck radius was 6.5 cm (2.5 in). Using the same centre, another circle, radius 9.5 cm (3.75 in) was drawn, and the vertical and horizontal axes were marked. On the outer circle and with a radius of 5 cm (2 in), six touching circles were drawn with their centres on the outer circle, starting at the centre back. There was a small gap at centre front.

A master pattern was prepared from my notebooks of Ottoman embroideries. Typical floral motifs were drawn, photocopied, reduced, reversed, inverted, linked, separated, rejected, cut out separately so I could see how they would fit into the collar scallops. Once I was satisfied, the motifs were glued onto the scallop outline and the whole taped onto a light box, with the fabric taped on top of that. The problem of constructing a smooth outline on the fabric without the use of the compass, (it can't be used on a lightbox)

This pattern has been reduced to fit the page. To reproduce it full size, enlarge it to 200% on a photocopier.

Method

The carnations and lilies were worked in double running stitch, with buttonhole and feather stitch details on the lilies. The outlines, in gold perle, were all in back stitch as it gives a smoother finish than double running. The small leaves were worked in satin stitch, and the larger ones in fishbone stitch. The entire background was worked in musabak stitch in metallic Madeira 300 machine thread.

✂ Work the floral motifs before the background

✂ Do not use more than 50 cm (20 in) of the thread in the needle at a time. Thread the needle from the end cut from the reel. Do not use a thimble as it wears the thread.

✂ Start the musabak stitch by running along the split stitch border edge. Finish the same way, or darn carefully into the back of the floral motifs.

✂ When you have established a good rhythm, it is easier to stitch around the irregular flower shapes. Work in both directions from the centre front, aiming to meet at a narrow place where it is easier to 'fudge' a few stitches if you must.

Finishing

To finish the scalloped edge, cut the excess fabric away a few centimetres at a time, half a centimetre (a quarter of an inch) from the split stitching. Turn the fabric under and, using white machine-cotton stitch over the split stitching. Then using Mercer crochet cotton No. 60, buttonhole stitch to cover all the previous foundation stitching. Be careful not to distort the scallops. When complete, trim away excess fabric from the back.

Finish with small gold sequins and gold leaves as shown. The musabak stitching makes the whole collar quite firm.

was circumvented by using a saucer and a lid that just happened to be the right size. Alternatively, a template of card could have been used. A waterproof pen was used for the outline.

The fabric was removed from the lightbox and the collar outlined in split stitch using a soft white perle cotton. Back on the lightbox, the floral motifs were outlined one at a time in pencil and carefully worked in a ring frame.

Conclusion

As I was completing this book, Donna Kennedy sent me her newest table scarf, saying that it had all the stitches on it that I had described in one of my classes. In this modern piece, all the characteristics of classical Ottoman embroidery are seen.

Here are the sprays of flowers rising from the small vases or urns, the tilt as the flowers waft in the breeze, the variety of blooms on the one stem, the out-of-scale trees, the border oh-so-close to the main field and the use of metallic thread.

Here, on specially woven fabric, are the knotted edges, the border with its alternating pink/red and blue/pale-blue flowers with rows of buttonhole stitch top and bottom.

The oversize roses, petals, calyx and sepals are in musabak stitch in rose pink, metallic gold and deep green respectively. The main stems are metallic gold satin stitch, and the outlines of petals and sepals in maroon and lime green respectively in dog tooth stitch, as are the 'hyacinths' above the roses. They are in the two shades of blue, as are the six little musabak stitch flowers in the spray directly above each maroon and gold vase.

The cypress trees have metallic gold Turkish triangular stitch trunks and musabak stitch foliage with edges of dog tooth stitch.

It is wonderful that this vibrant form of embroidery is still being produced today. It is still evolving and it is still collected, loved and used. Long may this continue!

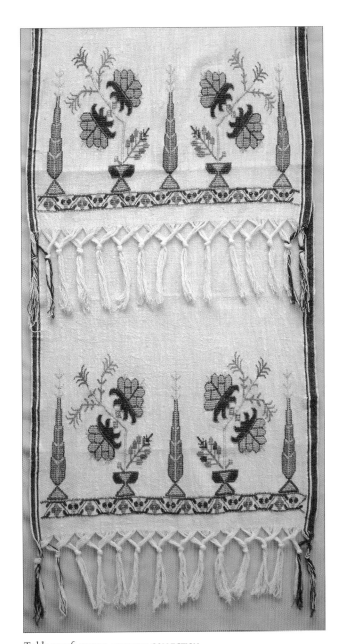

Table scarf. DONNA KENNEDY COLLECTION

Bibliography

de Bernieres, Louis. *Birds Without Wings*. Secker & Warburg, London, 2004.

Black, David. *Embroidered Flowers from Thrace to Tartary*. David Black Oriental Carpets, London, 1981.

Ellis, Marianne and Wearden, Jennifer. *Ottoman Embroidery*. V&A Publications, London, 2001.

Goodwin, Jason. *Lords of the Horizons: a History of the Ottoman Empire*. Chatto & Windus, London, 1998.

Gostelow, Mary. *Embroidery: Traditional Designs, Techniques and Patterns from All Over the World*. Marshall Cavendish, London, 1978.

Hogrefe, Jeffrey. *O'Keeffe: the Life of an American Legend*. Bantam Books, New York, 1992.

Krody, Sumru Belger. *Flowers of Silk & Gold: Four Centuries of Ottoman Embroidery*. Merrell (in association with The Textile Museum, Washington, D.C.), London, 2000.

Ramazanoglu, Gulseren. *Turkish Embroidery*. Van Nostrand Reinhold, London, 1976.

Stone, Caroline. *The Embroideries of North Africa*. Longman, Harlow, 1985.

Ther, Ulla. *Floral Messages: from Ottoman Court Embroideries to Anatolian Trousseau Chests*. Temmen, Bremen, 1993.

Victoria & Albert Museum. *Brief Guide to Turkish Woven Fabrics* (revised edition). Victoria & Albert Museum, London, 1950.

Victoria & Albert Museum and Johnstone, Pauline. *Turkish Embroidery*. Victoria & Albert Museum, London, 1985.

Wark, Edna. *Drawn Fabric Embroidery*. Batsford, London, 1979.

Various articles by Marianne Ellis published in *Embroidery UK*, 1989 and 1992.

Historical documents from The Textile Museum, Washington, D.C. including: 'Old Turkish Towels', *The Art Bulletin,* Vols 14 and 20, (1932 and 1938). The College Art Association of America.

Index

About the author

Beginning at about age four, there hasn't been a time when I did not stitch or knit. Family traditions of handwork came to New Zealand from England between 1832 and 1881 with my forebears, who brought with them a spirit of adventure and a philosophy of 'I can do it', as well as many practical skills.

I have always thought of myself as a 'transition woman', a true product of my age. First and foremost, I am a wife, mother and grandmother. School brought a love of art, forsaken to gain a science degree and to teach in secondary schools.

Like most young women of my generation, marriage in my twenties required a trousseau of embroidered linens sufficient to last several lifetimes. With the advent of children came a certain expertise in dressmaking, and also an inordinate amount of voluntary work in church and community.

In 1984 I joined the Auckland Embroiderers' Guild, and also began to study part time at Whitecliffe Art School, graduating with a Diploma in Textile Art in 1987. Since then, I have attended workshops by most of the overseas tutors who have visited New Zealand — from the UK, Lucy Goffin, Jeanette Durrant, Jane Lemon, Maggie Grey, Michael Brennand Wood and the late Constance Howard, and from the USA, Barbara Lee Smith, Jill Nordfors Clark, Tom Lundberg and Wilkie Smith.

A compulsive exhibitor, I have gained a sprinkling of awards and sold sufficient to local and overseas buyers to cover my costs. One of my pieces travelled New Zealand with the show *The Romance of Embroidery* and another was with the *New Zealand on Show* exhibition at the Voirrey Centre, UK. I have taught various forms of embroidery in New Zealand, as well as in the USA and in Canada.

Highlights of my artistic career would have to include: working on the Globe Theatre Curtains; commissioned works for St Lukes Presbyterian Church, Remuera, Auckland, and for the law firm Sellar Bone and Partners; countless clerical stoles, pulpit falls and banners; contributing two chapters to *Exploring Embroidery*, the first published embroidery book by New Zealanders; and being a finalist in the 1998 Telecom Book Cover Awards.

As the recipient of the 2000 ANZEG Travel Grant, I studied Ottoman Embroidery in Washington, DC. This study has expanded into a research project that has taken me down many interesting by-ways and through which I have made many wonderful friends.

After three years as Convener and Magazine Editor of The Combined Textiles Guild of NZ Inc., I self published *Ottoman (Turkish) Embroidery — A Journey of Discovery* in November 2003.

I love plants and gardens, colour and simple stitchery used in a painterly way.

The artistry of the Ottoman embroideries as it reflects the evolving lifestyles over four centuries of social development not only resonates for me but it provides a potential 'pole' with which to make a 'creative vault'. What if one of the intriguing outlines found in Ottoman embroidery was made large, of metal, with regular holes so a fabric of cord could be created within, and then 'stitched' with strips of silk in musabak or murver stitch? Imagine it hanging away from a wall, casting shadows on it! A prototype of woven cotton, cord and gold kid on a cane base, called 'Shield', (110 x 30 cm) was made for an exhibition in 2002.

The learning process continues.

Joyce I Ross
2005